THINKING  HIST

JON NICHOL

THE 1ST AND 2ND WORLD WARS

Contents

(Entries in bold type are National Curriculum headings.)

SIMON & SCHUSTER
EDUCATION

Roots

All of us have roots in the past, our own histories and those of our families. Our friends, neighbours and the people we work and go to school with also have their own family roots.

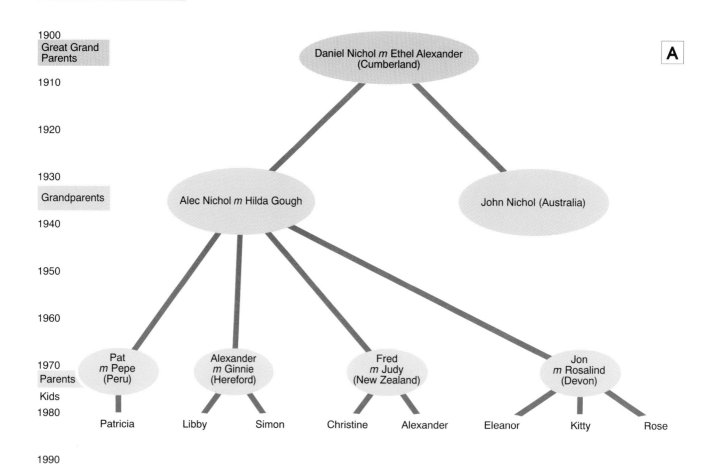

| 1900 Great Grand Parents |
| 1910 |
| 1920 |
| 1930 Grandparents |
| 1940 |
| 1950 |
| 1960 |
| 1970 Parents |
| Kids |
| 1980 |
| 1990 |

A

Daniel Nichol *m* Ethel Alexander (Cumberland)

Alec Nichol *m* Hilda Gough

John Nichol (Australia)

Pat *m* Pepe (Peru)

Alexander *m* Ginnie (Hereford)

Fred *m* Judy (New Zealand)

Jon *m* Rosalind (Devon)

Patricia

Libby   Simon

Christine   Alexander

Eleanor   Kitty   Rose

B

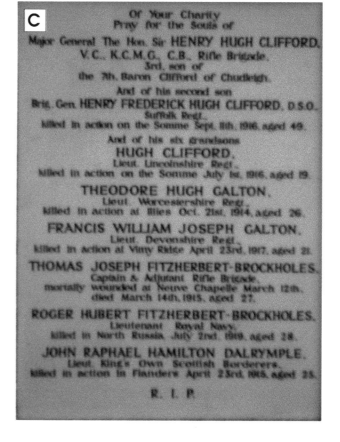

C

Of Your Charity
Pray for the Souls of
Major General The Hon. Sir HENRY HUGH CLIFFORD,
V.C., K.C.M.G., C.B., Rifle Brigade,
3rd. son of
the 7th. Baron Clifford of Chudleigh.
And of his second son
Brig. Gen. HENRY FREDERICK HUGH CLIFFORD, D.S.O.
Suffolk Regt.
killed in action on the Somme Sept. 11th. 1916. aged 49

And of his six grandsons
HUGH CLIFFORD,
Lieut. Lincolnshire Regt.
killed in action on the Somme July 1st. 1916. aged 19.

THEODORE HUGH GALTON,
Lieut. Worcestershire Regt.
killed in action at Illies Oct. 21st. 1914. aged 26.

FRANCIS WILLIAM JOSEPH GALTON,
Lieut. Devonshire Regt.
killed in action at Vimy Ridge April 23rd. 1917. aged 21.

THOMAS JOSEPH FITZHERBERT-BROCKHOLES,
Captain & Adjutant Rifle Brigade,
mortally wounded at Neuve Chapelle March 12th.
died March 14th. 1915. aged 27.

ROGER HUBERT FITZHERBERT-BROCKHOLES,
Lieutenant Royal Navy,
killed in North Russia July 2nd. 1919. aged 28.

JOHN RAPHAEL HAMILTON DALRYMPLE,
Lieut. King's Own Scottish Borderers.
killed in action in Flanders April 23rd. 1915. aged 25.

R. I. P.

• My family's roots go back a long way. Our relatives are now spread out all over the world (**A**).

• You have to ask questions to find out about the history of your own and other families.

• Two major events which most old people can tell you something about are the two world wars, the First World War (1914-18) and the Second World War (1939-45).

• What questions would you like to ask old people about them?

At home you might have pictures like **B**. All around you are signs of the impact of World War I, like **C**, which filled me with horror when I first saw it. Can you think why? Think how you would feel if all your brothers or boys you know were killed in a war. In one of my favourite history books I came across **D** which gave me clues about the impact of World War I on many families.

> *Then came the First World War. It took for a time all the able-bodied men out of the village and killed fifteen of them, but it was not so much their loss that affected village life as what the experiences of the war did to those who came back. New ideas, new attitudes, new horizons, new trades and occupations were revealed to them. The long-established order of society was no longer taken for granted. Jack was as good as his master or better. The motor-bike had been invented. Young men could go to work or go courting into the next county if that was where their fancy took them.* (**D**)

(Roland Parker, *The Common Stream*, 1976)

Family Scrapbook

You can start your own World War I family scrapbook to give you an idea about the impact of the First World War.

1 Finding out and asking questions (AT3, AT1)

a Work out a list of questions you would like to ask about the First World War.

b Ask your oldest relative or the oldest person you know about the First World War and the impact it had on their family.

c As a class, pool the information you receive.

d Make up a conversation between the figures in **B** about their thoughts, hopes and fears.

2 Roots (AT1)

a Draw a potato diagram like **A** of your own family for 1900-1990+.

b Mark on it the dates of the First World War and Second World War.

c Put potatoes on the diagram for any facts you have about your family in the World Wars - facts like those the Clifford family (see **C**) would put on its diagram .

3 Timeline (AT1)

a On a double page make out a timeline for World War I like the one below. Put years down the left-hand side, **The Western Front** at the top and **Consequences of the battles** at the bottom.

	The Western Front
1914	
1915	
1916	
1917	
1918	
Consequences of the battles	

b Put the following on your chart:

• an event which source **B** suggests

• the facts from source **C** about fighting in World War I

• three outcomes or consequences of the war mentioned in source **D**

• other things about World War I which you have found out in your research

3

The Western Front

Why did Britain join the First World War? Where was the Western Front? Who fought there? What did the fighting involve? Why did trench warfare start? When was there trench warfare? These are six key questions to ask about the Western Front. Here are some short and, I hope, clear and simple answers:

Why did Britain Join the First World War?

In August 1914 Germany marched into France through Belgium. Britain then declared war on Germany because she had promised to protect Belgium (see **A**). France was Britain's ally.

Where was the Western Front?

A small army, the British Expeditionary Force, was sent to France to fight alongside the French. The Western Front was in France (see **B**).

Who fought there?

On the Western Front the Allies - French and British forces - dug in in trenches and faced the Germans.

What did the fighting involve?

Troops fought from trenches across a wasteland of shell holes, mud and barbed wire. They mainly used rifles, machine-guns and heavy guns (artillery) which fired shells.

Why did trench warfare start?

During August and September 1914 (the first two months of the war between the British and French and the Germans) armies marched to and fro at will. The armies moved quickly and tried to beat each other in pitched battles. They soon found out that machine-guns, artillery and rapid rifle fire meant that an army which fought above ground would be wiped out. So, they dug in and created the trenches.

When was there trench warfare?

From September 1914 to March 1918 the armies

faced each other in trenches. Trench warfare ended in March 1918 when the Germans worked out how to break through the British and French lines. From March to November 1918 the war in the West was fought by the Germans advancing first and then the American, British and French forces pushing them back hundreds of kilometres.

To fight on the Western Front the British government had to raise a huge, mass army. The Western Front was part of a larger picture.
- Germany and her ally Austria-Hungary fought in **two** main places, the Western and Eastern Fronts. Russia was Germany's enemy in the East.
- War also raged in Italy, the Middle East, the colonies and at sea.
- In the West the war was one of deadlock, in the East it was one in which armies moved at will. Can you think why?
- By 1917 Germany had defeated Russia in the East

What might the war have meant for members of your family? **C** is a clue I found in a book for you to think about.

> *One morning I left home to go to work: we were repairing roads at the time, but on the way I met a friend who was going to enlist [join the army]. Instead of going on to work, I went back home, changed in to my best clothes and went with him to the recruiting office.* **(C)**

(quoted in Alan Lloyd, *The War in the Trenches*, Book Club Associates, 1976)

In a huge rush to enlist, whole streets, factories, clubs and groups of students joined up. Many were to die together in the living hell that was the Western Front.

War Poster

You can add a war poster to your scrapbook about the outbreak of the war.

1 Researching the poster - thinking about war (AT3, AT1)

a As if you were alive in August 1914 and you have just been told your country is at war, find out who Britain was fighting and why, what the British government was going to do about it and where a British army might go.

b Think about what you have heard people say about the war (there was no radio), and have read in the newspapers.

c What thoughts do you have about the Germans and the coming war?

d What message is the artist who drew **A** trying to get across?

e Your father or brother comes home and tells you he has enlisted (**C**). What thoughts flash through your mind? What feelings do you have? What might your mum and grandparents say?

f As a class you can pool ideas on the board.

2 Poster (AT2, AT1)

a Design the poster to include as many points as you can about why Britain went to war and why men should enlist to fight.

b Put up your posters as a classroom display.

c Compare the posters and the messages they are trying to get across.

The Home Front, 1914-18

What might the First World War have meant to your family? Think of at least three questions about the First World War that you would like answered? To help you answer such questions I picked out clues **A** and **I** from books on the war and **B-H** from a local newspaper. **A** is a famous historian's account of what the war meant to the people in the town where I live, Exeter, Devon. There should be history books like it of your local town or city.

In this fortunate country we never heard a shot fired in anger. But all the same there were wounded soldiers in their hospital-blue suits limping everywhere, and in the years 1916 and 1917 there were few homes that had not lost a man in battle, or who had not some maimed survivor.

By the early months of 1917 food was becoming scarce in the towns. The German submarine campaign was taking a very heavy toll of ships bringing food to Britain. In the early weeks of 1917 it was even impossible to find any potatoes in the towns. Some families could get none for a week at a time. If a shop had some potatoes, the police were called to control the hungry crowds who queued for them. Butter, when one could find it, sold for 1s 10d to 2s a pound [9-10p for 500 g], eggs had reached the fantastic price (for those days) of 2s 3d to 2s 6d [11-12½p] a dozen. Everything had at least doubled in price, although wages had also risen... **(A)**

(W.G. Hoskins, *Devon and its People*, 1959)

Food Concessions
respecting Butchers' Meat, Bacon and Ham
The food controller has issued an order which comes into effect on and from tomorrow, by which all bacon may be sold free of coupons. Holders of ration books are not permitted to change their dealer... Not less than 8 ounces [220 g] of bacon, or 12 ounces [340 g] of ham, are to be supplied per week per customer if demanded. **(B)**

St Thomas (East) [Exeter]
War Weapons Week
Below is a list of the parishes in St. Thomas' East Area which took part in the War Weapons Week Campaign from July 13th to 20th, together with the amount raised in each case... Silverton over £10 per head... **(C)**

Soldiers and Christians
Newton Abbot Tailor and His Conscience
James Hancock, Tailor, 32, applied on conscientious grounds and said that for thirty years it had been his conviction that he would not, as a Christian, become a soldier, and he could not engage in military training, or be armed with any weapon for the taking of human life, as it would be inconsistent, as a Christian, for him to do so.
Mr G.D. Woolacombe: 'Are you willing to undertake other work of national importance?'
Hancock: 'My present position is a certified one - wholesale tailoring'.
... Hancock said he had no objection to doing ambulance work.
Major Oswald-Brown: 'I should hope not, good Lord!' **(D)**

For Tommy and Jack
Scheme to Provide Land on Return to Their Former Homes
With the object of enabling discharged soldiers from country parishes on their return to their former homes to obtain a piece of land for cultivation on a voluntary basis, a scheme has been devised by the Central Land Association. (The land to be) plots or a little field of five acres or thereabouts close to the cottage in which the demobilised soldier or sailor lives. **(E)**

Roll of Honour
West-Country Casualties in Recent Fighting
Pte. F. Parson (Exeter) Middlesex Regiment is officially reported to have died of wounds; L.J. Brealy (Bovey Tracey), Wiltshire Regiment, and Lance-Corpl. N.F Mardon (Dartmouth) Worcester

Regiment, to be wounded. Mr. A. Bellringer, of 32, Radford-road, Exeter, has received a post card from the Red Cross Order of St. John stating that his son, Private F. C. Bellringer, 2nd, Devon, is a prisoner of war in Germany and is well. He was reported missing on May 25th last. **(F)**

Why Fruit Stones and Nutshells are Wanted

Fruit stones and hard nutshells are urgently demanded by the Government for conversion into charcoal, which is to be used in the British respirator for the protection of our troops against poison gas. The urgency of the need will be seen from the fact that at present no other substance is known to give equal protection. **(G)**

The Germans used submarines to try and starve Britain into surrender. The British government tried to bring in rationing to share out what food there was (see **B**).

It struck me that, as nearly all men between 18-45 years old were in the army, most women had to run single parent families. How do you think they coped in an age before fridges, washing machines and tumble driers? With the men away, women took over many of their jobs too. **H** gives you a clue about what this meant. Women played such a huge part in the war effort that when peace came the government was at last persuaded to give them the vote.

When the war ended in November 1918, Exeter ground to a halt:

In all the towns the main streets were solid with people. Everybody had left his or her job, in office, shop, workshop or factory, to process up and down until it was impossible to move a foot. Schoolboys formed bands with pots and pans and marched around where they could. There was cheering and dancing. **(I)**

(W.G. Hoskins, *Devon and its People*, 1959)

The woman in the picture belongs to the land army which took over men's jobs in farming.

The Trenches

Do you keep a diary? Have you read the diary of Adrian Mole? How about creating a First World War diary? Luckily we have lots of such diaries to help us. My favourite is that of Siegfried Sassoon, published as *Memoirs of A Fox-Hunting Man* and *Memoirs of an Infantry Officer*. I first read it when I was your age.

If you were a man aged between 18 and 45, you would receive a letter telling you to report to barracks. Mum and dad would see you off with tears in their eyes from your local station. At the barracks you would report to the guardhouse. The sergeant would send you to the stores, where you would get your uniform, rifle and the rest of the equipment (see **B**). From the stores you would stagger to your new home, a room with twenty or thirty other soldiers. Most of your time would be spent in marching, learning how to fire and clean your rifle and to charge the enemy with your bayonet.

If you don't kill him, he'll kill you ... stick him between the eyes, in the throat, in the chest. **(A)**

(war instructor's advice)

B

Gasmask

Ammunition pouches for bullets

Cape

Grenades

Waterbottle

Shovel

Boots

Rifle

Haversack

Helmet

Eating tin

Bayonet

Puttees

Write out a list of the soldier's clothes and equipment. By each item say what it would have been used for.

Some days you would leave the barracks and camp in the countryside, where you might mount guard:

There was, I remember, a low mist lying on the fields, and I was posted by a gate under a walnut tree. In the autumn smelling silence the village church clanged one o'clock. Shortly afterwards I heard someone moving in my direction across the field which I was facing. ... Holding my rifle defensively (and a loaded rifle too) I remarked in an unemphatic voice: 'Halt, who goes there?' There was no reply. Out of the mist and the weeds through which it was wading emerged the Kentish cow which I had challenged. **(C)**

(Siegfried Sassoon, *Memoirs of A Fox-Hunting Man*)

While training you might hear from your best friend who had joined up and gone to the front, and who writes to you each week. No letter, and then you hear he 'has been killed in action'. All the time you think about what it will be like to fight. Then orders arrive for you to leave for France. A weekend at home, mum and dad see you off, the real thing this time:

What did they say to one another ... when the train had snorted away and left an empty space in front of them? **(D)**

(Siegfried Sassoon, *Memoirs of A Fox-Hunting Man*)

Across the channel to France, next a train journey to the front line. From the train you march to where you will live and fight. Time is split between the trenches in the front line and the base camp – six days in the trenches, four days out. Here are some extracts from Sassoon's diaries about life in a trench like **E** which is part of the front line, as described in **F**. The first thing to think about is that you were filthy, unwashed for days or weeks and smothered in lice, with no clean clothes.

Being in the trenches meant, among other things, having a 'trench mouth' (mouth ulcers).

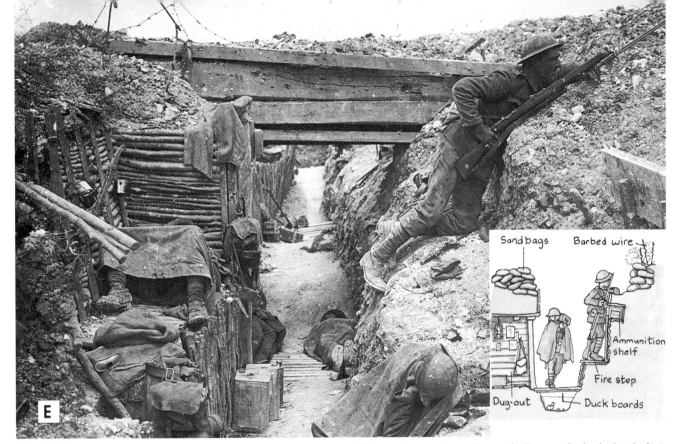

E

Sandbags Barbed wire

Ammunition
shelf

Fire step

Dug-out Duck boards

I can see myself sitting in the sun in a nook among the sandbags and chalky debris… There is a strong smell of chloride of lime. I am scraping the caked mud off my wire-torn puttees with a rusty entrenching tool… A little weasel runs past my outstretched feet, glancing at me with tiny bright eyes. [Shells pass over head, a shrapnel shell goes off over the German line.] Against the clear morning sky a cloud of dark smoke expands and drifts away. **(F)**

(Siegfried Sassoon, *Memoirs of an Infantry Officer*)

This is a famous picture of a trench. Can you think why I picked it?

At night you might lay wire or go on raids. Day in and day out, week in and week out, exploding shells and mine, poison gas, rifle and machine-gun fire kill the men around you, one by one. You are waiting for the big push, the battle which will defeat the Germans and make it all worthwhile.

World War Diary

You can create your own diaries or poems and read them out and/or display them.

1 Researching, thinking and questioning (AT3, AT1)
a Find out what you can about the trenches.
b How would you feel:
• when training and being given the instructions in **A**?
• mounting guard when the events described in **C** happened?
• leaving home for the last time (see **D**)?
• living in the trenches as in **E** and **F**?
c Jot down three facts about both **E** and **F** and three

things you could hear, smell, taste and feel in the trenches.
d As a group or class, pool your ideas.

2 Writing your diary or poem (AT2, AT1)
Write or record your own diary entry for the following or a poem about one of them:
• hearing about the outbreak of war
• being called up, leaving home, first day in the barracks
• training, friend's death
• leaving for the front
• crossing the channel, journey to the front line
• life in the trenches

3 Read out, play or display your diaries or poems (AT2)
Talk about the ways in which they are the same and the ways in which they differ.

ACTIVITY · ACTIVITY

The Somme

BRITISH NEWSFLASH

7.30 a.m. 31 June 1916. The war in the West has settled down into a killing match between the British and French and the Germans. At Verdun the French are holding out against a huge German attack. Thousands are dying daily.

The British are about to attack on the Somme to force the Germans to take men away from the Verdun front. On the Somme 400,000 British men face about 50,000 Germans. The Germans are dug in in fortified villages (see **A**). Their trenches are well planned and run in lines for miles. For a week over 400 British heavy guns have smashed the German trenches and blown their wire to bits. The shelling has been at its heaviest for the last day and has just stopped.

A huge mine has just gone off under the German lines **(B)**. Whistles blow and our men clamber out of their trenches–they are going over the top **(C)**. I can see waves of British troops slowly walking forwards. They are carrying up to 80 pounds (36 kg) of ammunition and equipment. A walk over – our shells, gas, air attacks and mines have killed all the Germans.

This is the greatest German defeat in history. Victory is ours!

GERMAN NEWSFLASH

4.00 p.m. 2 July 1916 General Haig, the British commander, informs us that the British troops have failed to take our German fortified villages. Over 57,000 British men have been lost; 19,000 of these are dead, 35,000 wounded, 3000 captured.

During the shelling we took shelter in deep, shell-proof shelters. When the shelling stopped our men climbed back into their trenches and set up their machine-guns **(D)** and rifles. An officer told me:

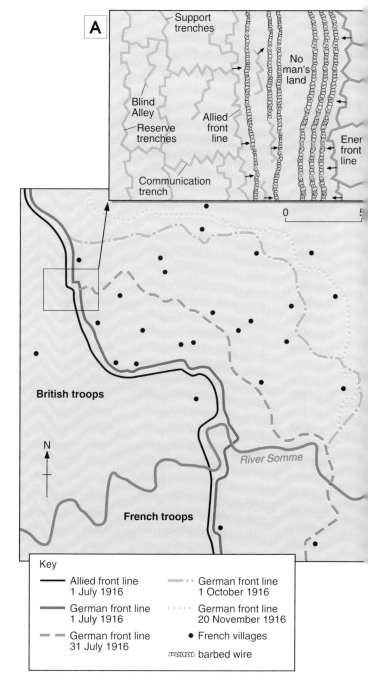

A

Support trenches

No man's land

Blind Alley

Allied front line

Reserve trenches

Ener front line

Communication trench

0   5

British troops

N

River Somme

French troops

Key

— Allied front line 1 July 1916

– German front line 1 July 1916

– – German front line 31 July 1916

-·-·- German front line 1 October 1916

······· German front line 20 November 1916

• French villages

⟳⟳⟳ barbed wire

B

C

A picture taken from a film made a few weeks later in Britain to show how the troops went over the top at the Battle of the Somme.

66 *As soon as we were ready a series of long lines of British infantry were seen moving forward from their trenches. The first line seemed to go on without end from left to right. A second line, then a third and fourth followed the first line. They came on at a steady pace, as if expecting to find nothing alive in our front trenches. A few seconds later, the rattle of machine-gun and rifle fire broke out from our whole line. Whole sections appeared to fall. All along the line, Englishmen could be seen throwing their arms into the air and collapsing, never to move again. Badly wounded rolled about in their agony, while other casualties crawled into shell holes for shelter... With all this were mingled the moans of the wounded, cries for help and the last screams of death. Again and again the lines of British infantry broke against the German defences like waves against a cliff, only to be beaten back. It was an amazing sight of great bravery.* 99 **(E)**

(German officer's report on the British attack on the Somme)

D

This is the greatest British defeat in history. Victory is ours!

The Somme! Newspaper

You can create a front page for either the British or the German newsflash. Your secret service will have given you a copy of the enemy newsflash, but you do not have to believe it. Work on your own, in pairs or threes.

Planning and designing (AT1, AT2)

For each newsflash include the following:
• a headline giving news of the attack
• a plan of the front line, showing how the British had prepared for the attack
• an idea of how strong the German position is
• an idea of how well the British will be able to fight
• the impact of the shelling by the British heavy guns, the state of the barbed wire, the impact it has had on the Germans
• the explosion of the mine
• the British going over the top and how well they have done

ACTIVITY · ACTIVITY

Oh What A Lovely War!

We hear about war all the time. I bet that when you open a comic or magazine or switch on the radio or TV something about war will come up. *Oh What A Lovely War* was a famous show about World War I. You can use things such as poems, songs and paintings like **A-D** to produce your own show on World War I. **A-D** made a big impact on me when I first came across them.

  'Good-morning; good-morning!' the General said
When we met him last week on our way to the line.
Now the soldiers he smiled at are most of 'em dead,
And we're cursing his staff for incompetent swine.
'He's a cheery old card,' grunted Harry to Jack
As they slogged up to Arras with rifle and pack.
     *   *   *   *   *

But he did for them both by his plan of attack.
(A)

(Siegfried Sassoon)

And now a song for you to sing (to the tune of Holy, Holy, Holy!):

  Raining, raining, raining, always bloody well raining.
Raining all the morning, and raining all the day.
Grousing, grousing, grousing, always bloody well grousing,
Grousing at the weather and grousing at the pay.
(B)

Read poem **C** out loud to get across what it was like to be in a gas attack, and act out what happened to the dying man:

  Gas! Gas! Quick, boys! - an ecstasy of fumbling
Fitting the clumsy helmets just in time.
But someone still was yelling out and stumbling
And flound'ring like a man in fire or lime.
Dim through the misty panes and thick green light
As under a green sea, I saw him drowning.
In all my dreams before my helpless sight
He plunges at me, guttering, choking,
  drowning. **(C)**

(Wilfred Owen, war poet, died in action on the Western Front)

D is part of a painting which covers the walls of a tiny little chapel in Sussex. As a statement about the horror of war, I found it very moving.

The First World War Show

As a class you can produce your own First World War show. You will either speak, sing, act or mime it.

1 Researching and thinking (AT3)
a Find as many World War I songs, poems, stories, pictures and paintings as you can. Think hard about the point of view they are trying to get across.
b Look at **D**.
• Take any one part of the picture and describe in detail what is going on.
• Then say what you think was going through Stanley Spencer's mind when he painted that part of the picture.
• Discuss all the parts of the picture.
• Then try and work out what the artist's message is about the First World War.

2 Deciding and finding out (AT3, AT1)
a Look at pages 12-13 and decide what topics you would like to include in the show.
b Split the topics up among members of the class.
c Decide what approach you will take in putting on the show.
d Decide how you will present your topic, e.g. a poem, song, play, mime, a spoken account.
e Work out what kind of scenery or backcloth you might like (see **D**) and draw up a design for it.

3 Writing and presenting your piece (AT2, AT1)
a Either on your own or in a pair or group, write your piece.
b Rehearse it for presenting to the rest of the class as part of your First World War show.
c As a class plan out the show.
d Present your piece as part of the show.

1918 – Victory

If you keep your eyes open you will see in every English town, village and church monuments to men who were slaughtered in the trenches between 1914 and 1918 (see **B**). On one may well be the names of your great grandfathers. In 1917 Siegfried Sassoon was wounded and sent home to recover. Letters from his friends at the front were full of news of the soldiers he had fought alongside in the trenches:

I am sorry to say that the Padre got killed... He was up with the lads in the very front and got sniped in the stomach and died immediately. I haven't much room for his crowd as a rule, but he was the finest parson I've ever known... Young Brock... was engaging the Boche single-handed when he was badly hit in the arm, side, and leg. They amputated his left leg, but he was too far gone and we buried him today. Two other officers killed and three wounded. Poor Sergeant Blaxton was killed. All the best get knocked over. **(A)**

(quoted in Siegfried Sassoon, *Memoirs of an Infantry Officer*)

By 1917 the war was drifting along in a bloody stalemate, but during the year two events changed its course:

• The Russian armies stopped fighting the Germans in October 1917 when the Bolsheviks, or communists, seized power in Russia with their slogan 'Peace, Bread and Land'.
• America came into the war on Britain and France's side.

The war was now at crisis point. Would the Germans be able to use their troops from the Russian front to break through on the Western Front before huge numbers of Americans arrived? Or would the Americans swing the war in favour of the Allies?

In a race against time the Germans were the first to get ready. In **C** and **D**, which are taken from my GCSE History book, I summed up what happened.

March 1918 - November 1918: the War of Mobility

It is easy to forget that the Germans lost the First World War in a series of battles in 1918 that were as decisive as the Battle of Waterloo. These were battles of attack and counter-attack, and the rapid movement of large numbers of men. By March 1918 the generals had managed to work out a method of breaking the deadlock of trench warfare.

...with Russia knocked out, the Germans could pour men and resources in to the Western Front.

The Ludendorff Offensive
The German generals worked out a new approach to trench warfare. They would concentrate their artillery and gas attack on a few weak spots in the enemy lines. After a ferocious barrage of concentrated fire, they would then attack with specially trained storm-troopers, using flame-throwers, grenades and light machine-guns. This approach would punch gaping holes through the enemy lines, and the German forces could then encircle the enemy forces and attack them from the rear.

On 21 March Ludendorff attacked, broke through the British and French lines and advanced rapidly to the Marne. The armies of the Allies retreated before the onslaught, defeated but not broken. With the arrival of 50,000 fresh American troops a week, and learning from the German tactics, the Allied armies got ready to counter-attack. Under the single command of the Frenchman Foch they aimed to attack the Germans from three sides - from the front and on two flanks, for the German forces had formed a huge bulge into France.

The Counter-Attack

In July, the French counter-attacked on the Marne, and in early August the British army joined the assault with over 450 tanks. In a series of sweeping victories the Allies routed the German armies, which retreated to a line of fortifications, the Hindenburg Line. 🍳 **(C)**

(Sean Lang and Jon Nichol, *Work Out Modern World History*, Macmillan, 1990)

The war was over. Memorials like **B** were put up to remember those who would never speak again.

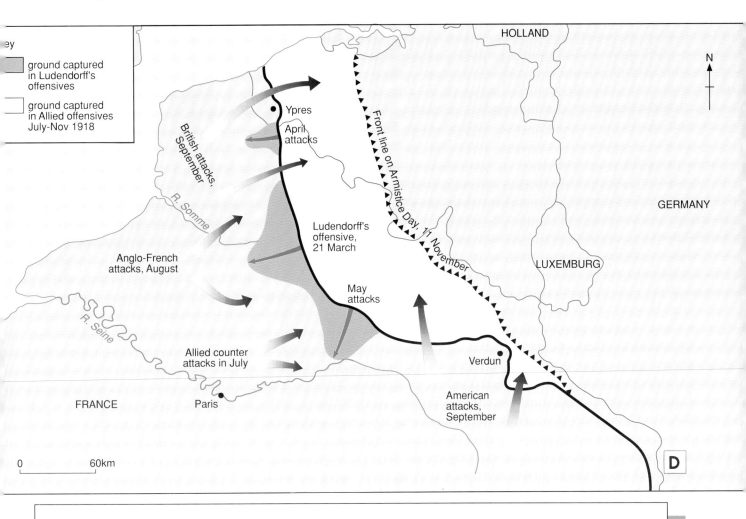

Monument!

Design your own monument to the dead of the First World War.

1 Research (AT3)

a The monument will reflect what your thoughts are on the First World War, and the message you want to get across.
b Read with care pages 14-15 and say what things you want to include on your monument (for example, a map of the final campaign, a picture or statue of a dead soldier, a symbol of peace).

2 Design (AT2)

a In rough, sketch out your ideas for a monument, marking the points you want to make on your drawing.
b In turn, explain your ideas to the rest of the class or members of your group.
c Change your design in response to comments made.

3 The Monument (AT2, AT1)

Produce a neat design of your monument, with notes and an account of the ideas that you are trying to get across.

ACTIVITY · ACTIVITY ·

Era of World War II

It was a bit of a shock. The guide was telling us all about the horrors of the Siege of Leningrad, see page 47, when one of the Russians asked our students what they knew about the Second World War. Out of twenty not one could say when it was and they didn't have a clue about who fought whom. All twenty had done A level History! The History National Curriculum believes that you should all know something about World War II because it has shaped the world you live in. To 'think' history you have to ask questions, so let us start off with three simple ones about the National Curriculum History Study Unit - **The Era of the Second World War.**

- When was the Second World War?
- What went on in it?
- Whom did it involve?

Spike Milligan (see inside front cover) can help us with one of these questions. I spotted that his book *Adolf Hitler, My Part in his Downfall* opens:

HOW IT ALL STARTED September 3rd, 1939. The last minutes of peace ticking away. Father and I were watching Mother digging our air-raid shelter. 'She's a great little woman', said Father. 'And getting smaller all the time,' I added. Two minutes later, a man called Chamberlain who did Prime Minister impressions spoke on the wireless; he said, 'As from eleven o'clock we are at war with Germany.' (I loved the WE) 'War?' said Mother. 'It must have been something we said', said Father. The people next door panicked, burnt their post office books and took in the washing. **(A)**

England went to war with Germany because the Germans had attacked Poland, and we had promised to fight on Poland's side if this happened. The Germans stormed into Poland with tanks and planes and quickly seized control of the country. **B** is a clue of what this meant for Poles. I chose **C** from a book I use to get the facts clear in my own head. **C** should help you to

make sense of what went on in the first three years of the war.

(i) Opening moves: September 1939 to December 1940. By the end of September the Germans and Russians had defeated and occupied Poland. After a five-month pause (known as the 'phoney war'), the Germans took over Denmark and Norway (April 1940); a British attempt to dislodge them failed and caused Chamberlain to be replaced as Prime Minister by Winston Churchill, who proved to be as outstanding a war leader as Lloyd George in the First World War. In May Germany attacked Holland, Belgium and France, who were soon defeated, leaving Britain alone to face the dictators (Mussolini had declared war in June, just before the fall of France). Hitler's attempt to bomb Britain into submission was thwarted in the Battle of Britain (July to September), but Mussolini's armies invaded Egypt and Greece.

(ii) **The Axis offensive widens: 1941 to the summer of 1942.** *The war now began to develop into a world-wide conflict. First Hitler, confident of victory over Britain, launched an invasion of Russia (June 1941), breaking the non-aggression pact signed less than two years previously; then the Japanese forced the USA into the war by attacking the American naval base at Pearl Harbor (December 1941) and proceeded to occupy the British territories of Malaya, Singapore and Burma, as well as the Philippine Islands. At this stage of the war there seemed to be no way of stopping the Germans and Japanese, though the Italians were less successful.*

(iii) **The offensives held in check: summer 1942 to summer 1943.** *This phase of the war saw three important battles in which Axis forces were defeated. In June 1942 the Americans drove off a Japanese attack on Midway Island, inflicting heavy losses. In October the Germans advancing into Egypt, were halted by the British at El Alamein and later driven out of North Africa. The third battle was in Russia where, by September 1942, the Germans had penetrated as far as Stalingrad. Here the Russians put up such a fierce resistance that the following February the German army was surrounded and compelled to surrender. Meanwhile the war in the air continued with both sides bombing enemy cities, and at sea, where, as in the First World War, the British and Americans gradually got the better of the German submarine menace.* (C)

(Norman Lowe, *Mastering Modern British History*, Macmillan 1984)

The final question we should ask is:

• What caused the Second World War?

We will start to look at this question on pages 18-29 and search out some answers from pages 30-31.

Timeline

To help make sense of this chapter you can create a timeline for **'Era'**, stretching from 1910-1950. You can put key facts from this page on the **Era** timeline and add others as you work through this book and find out new things.

1 Research (AT3, AT1)

a Note the year of your birth and try and find out when your grandparents and great grandparents were born. Ask them what they think were the most important things that have happened in their lifetimes with dates.

b Put all these facts and dates on your timeline, and add these to it: 1914-18 The First World War, 1939-45 The Second World War.

c From the contents list at the front of the book choose one heading that interests you. Read the chapter, and put down one or more things or facts to add to your **Era** timeline.

d Think of three questions you would like answered about the Second World War. Say how you think you might find the answers. As a class you can pool your questions.

2 Era timeline - sorting out facts (AT1, AT3)

a Put **Era Timeline** as the title of your work.

b Down the side put the dates 1910, 20, 30, 40 and 50, equally spaced out.

c Split the page into three columns headed Britain, Europe and Asia.

d Put your thoughts about **B**, key facts taken from **A** and **C** and any other facts you know into the three columns.

e Against key dates put the facts that you have found out about the period (see section **1 Research**).

f Add to your timeline as you work through this book.

The Peace Settlement

'Fight! Fight!' We all swarmed around the punching, kicking boy and girl. What was the fight about and who was to blame? We will never know, for when caught the boy and girl told a different story and each called the other a liar. It's just the same with the causes of the Second World War. Today nearly all of us say that Hitler, Germany's ruler from 1933, was to blame for war breaking out in 1939. But you can bet that if Germany had won the war we would all learn that Churchill, England's leader, caused the war. Can you think why?

But, we can all agree that what happened to Germany after the First World War (1914-18) had a big part to play in causing World War II twenty years later. What do you think **A** suggests? It is one of the most haunting cartoons I know. In 1919 the leaders of America, Britain and France who had beaten Germany met at Versailles near Paris to make peace. What did they do to Germany? To help you find out, I put in map **B** and the *Factfile*.

PEACE AND FUTURE CANNON FODDER

The Tiger: "Curious! I seem to hear a child weeping!"

Cartoon, 1919. The men shown are the leaders of Britain, Italy, France and America. Children who were babies in 1919 would be the soldiers of 1940.

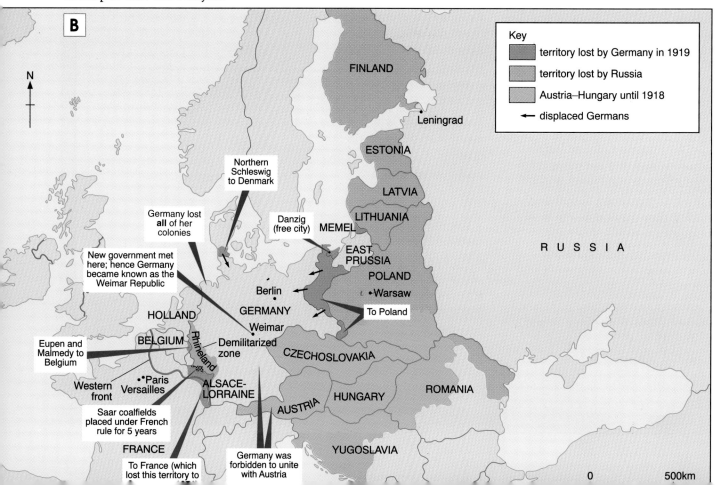

1914 – 18
• Vicious trench warfare on the Western Front.
• Germany defeats Russia and forces her to give up huge amounts of land early in 1918.
• By November 1918 America, Britain and France had beaten Germany.

	Population	War dead	Cost
Britain	41 million	750,000	Hundreds of ships sunk
France	40 million	1,400,000	300,000 homes wrecked
Germany	65 million	2,000,000	Widespread famine

Allied Demands
• **America's** president, Woodrow Wilson, wanted to make sure that Germany was never a threat again.
• Wilson wanted new nations to be set up in Eastern Europe.
• Wilson wanted a new world body, the League of Nations, which would keep the peace.
• In **Britain** the papers screamed for German blood and money, with cries of 'Hang the Kaiser' and 'Make Germany Pay'.
• The **French** leader, Clemenceau, wanted revenge, money to pay for war damage and the end of any threat from Germany's army.

• America, Britain and France, wanted to stop Russian communism, Bolshevism, from being a threat. The Bolsheviks wanted a communist revolution in Britain and the rest of Europe.

1919
Germany was forced to accept the Treaty of Versailles.

Terms of the Treaty
1 Land
• In the West Germany lost Alsace-Lorraine to France (see map **B**).
• In the East huge areas of land were lost to the new country of Poland.
• Austria-Hungary and western Russia were carved up into new countries.

2 Armed Forces
• Germany's army was slashed to 100,000 men.
• Germany was allowed no tanks, planes or submarines, and was only allowed six battleships.
• No German troops were allowed in the Rhineland. (Without control of the Rhine bridges, Germany would find it hard to invade France.)

3 War Guilt Clause
The Allies forced Germany to accept she was to blame for the First World War.

4 Payments
Germany was to pay a huge sum of money for war damage.

Cartoon

If cartoons are drawn with care and thought they can help you understand a lot of history. Here you are asked to draw a cartoon from *either* a British *or* a German point of view in 1919.

1 Sorting out ideas (AT3, AT1)
The British viewpoint is that of a family which had lost a father and his two brothers in the First World War. The German viewpoint is that of a soldier who had been gassed and seen most of his friends killed on the Western Front.
a Make out a table with your thoughts on how they would feel about the points below. First give the English view and then the German view and say why the point might be a cause of war twenty years later.
• German loss of land
• savage cuts in the German army, navy and airforce

• Germans being forced to accept the blame for the First World War and all the deaths and destruction caused (War Guilt Clause)
• Germany having to pay for all the war damage, for example, for ruined French farms and villages and sunk British shipping
b Look carefully at **A**. What messages is the artist trying to get across? What do you think his view is of the Versailles Settlement?

2 Drawing your cartoon (AT2)
You can work in pairs, one doing a German, the other a British cartoon.
a Plan out your cartoon to include all of the points which might lead to war, and then draw it.
b Swap cartoons and talk about the ideas they are putting across.
c You can put up a wall display of cartoons, German on one side, British on the other.

The Crash and Depression

Eleanor told me about her class being in trouble with their class teacher. They had all been mucking about and giggling because Jane had poked her friend Alice with a ruler. Alice then pushed Sharon off her chair as Sharon was always causing trouble and Alice thought it was Sharon's ruler that had prodded her. So, Sharon shouted at Alice, and a fight was about to break out. The teacher had got mad at them, and the whole class had all had to stay in at break. Who was to blame for the form staying in? List all the causes you can think of and put them in order of importance. You can see something that seems simple all at once becomes very complex. Think how much harder it is to work out what the causes were of the Second World War!

One factor was **the Depression** of the 1930s which lasted until the Second World War. In 1929 there was a world-wide banking crisis, **the Crash**. Think what would happen if banks had to shut down and there was no money to pay wages or for firms to keep going. Something like this happened in 1929. The result was the Depression in which firms, factories and shops closed, trade fell sharply, and unemployment soared. **A** shows the impact of the Depression on Germany. Can you see a link between these figures and Hitler coming to power in 1933 (**B**)? Hitler was the Nazi ruler of Germany.

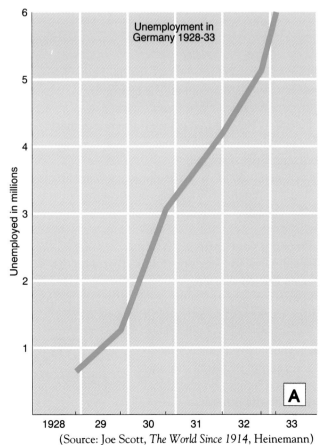

(Source: Joe Scott, *The World Since 1914*, Heinemann)

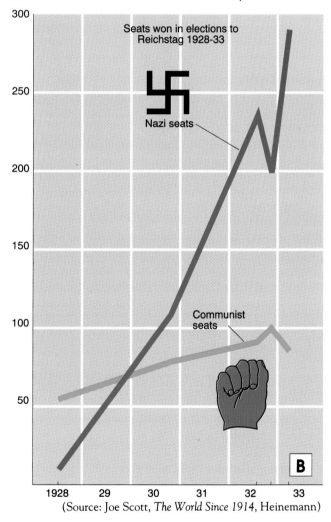

(Source: Joe Scott, *The World Since 1914*, Heinemann)

In 1939 the Second World War broke out between Hitler's Germany and Britain and France. At the same time Japan had gone to war in China. In 1941 Japan attacked America. America joined the fight against Germany.

A.J.P. Taylor, a famous historian, gives his view of the impact which the Depression had on the outbreak of war in 1939. I hope you can use what a real historian writes to sort out your own ideas:

> 66 *World trade declined catastrophically. There was mass unemployment - over two million in Great Britain, six million in Germany, fifteen million in the United States... Faced with this storm [countries waged economic war on each other]... At first a war of all against all, it soon changed its character and reinforced the division of the world... Some great powers - the United States most of all but also the British and the French empires - could, if pressed, make do on their own resources. Germany and Japan lost out. Though they, too, were great industrial nations, they could not provide for themselves. They needed raw materials from the rest of the world, yet the Depression made it impossible for them to obtain these by the normal methods of international trade.[Their leaders believed in autarky, i.e. they must set up their own economic empires.] The Japanese took the simplest course and [conquered] Manchuria [part of China] and then [the coastal areas of China]...*

> *When Hitler became ruler of Germany in January 1933, he embraced autarky as a positive good. Men debated later whether Hitler and the Nazis that he led were created by Versailles or the Depression. The answer is by both. Economic discontent carried Hitler to power, but he had already established his reputation by his campaign against Versailles. In his view, the German Depression was the legacy [result] of defeat... Autarky would strengthen Germany for political conquests, and these would in turn enable her to carry autarky further.* 99 **(C)**

(A.J.P. Taylor, *The Second World War*, Hamish Hamilton/ Rainbird, 1975)

Causation Chart

You can make out a chart to show how the Depression helped lead to war in 1939.

1 Working on the sources (AT3)
Study the sources, and choose which point you think is most likely to be true for each question.
a Using **A**, in which year was an extreme party, which promised to solve all of Germany's problems, likely to do best?

   1928   1929   1930   1931   1932

b Using **B**, in which year were the Nazis most popular?

   1928   1929   1930   1931   1932

c Compare **A** and **B**. Do they suggest that the Depression was:
• the only reason for Nazi support?
• one of several reasons?
d Read through **C** quickly. Suggest what its main idea is. Work out the meaning of words and phrases you do not know. Copy out the sentence or sentences in **C** which support your answer to **c**.
e What did America, Britain, Germany and Japan do because of the Depression?
• cooperate
• nothing
• wage economic war on each other
f Germany and Japan said that to survive they had to:
• do nothing
• support free trade
• set up their own economic empires

g Why did Germany and Japan behave in this way?
• because they had too many raw materials in their country
• because they did not have enough raw materials in their country
• because they had just enough raw materials in their country
h Japan solved its problems through
• doing nothing
• free trade
• conquering Manchuria and the Chinese coast
i Germany thought that autarky would help
• make her rich
• conquer other countries
• support free trade between her and other countries
j There are several ways in which the Depression helped to cause the Second World War. Choose one or more of the following:
• short-term cause
• immediate cause
• long-term cause
• direct cause
• indirect cause
• important cause
• unimportant cause

2 Chart (AT1)
Make out a chart with the title, **The Great Depression and the Causes of World War II**. Write out each question or a heading from **a-j** with your answer.

ACTIVITY · ACTIVITY ·

Communism, Fascism and Democracy

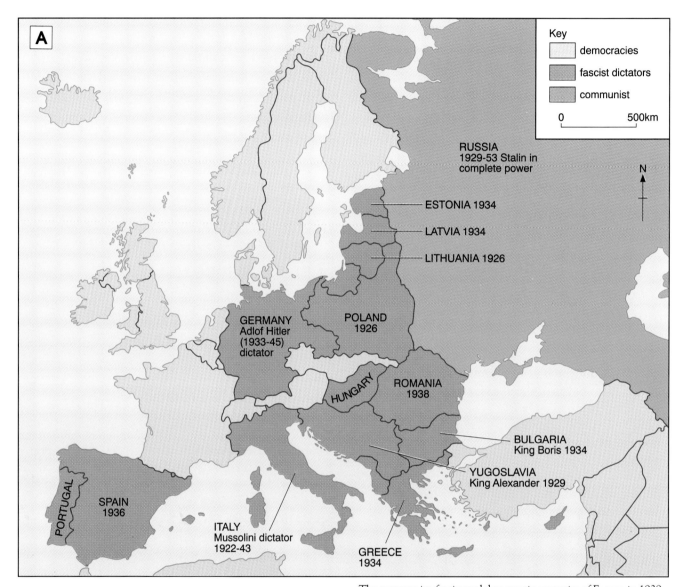

Key	
	democracies
	fascist dictators
	communist

0   500km

A

RUSSIA
1929-53 Stalin in
complete power

ESTONIA 1934

LATVIA 1934

LITHUANIA 1926

GERMANY
Adlof Hitler
(1933-45)
dictator

POLAND
1926

HUNGARY

ROMANIA
1938

BULGARIA
King Boris 1934

YUGOSLAVIA
King Alexander 1929

PORTUGAL

SPAIN
1936

ITALY
Mussolini dictator
1922-43

GREECE
1934

The communist, fascist and democratic countries of Europe in 1939.

'Communist pig', 'Fascist swine', '*Guardian* [a newspaper] reading pinko' are phrases of abuse you might hear in a fierce political row. From 1917 to the present day the ideas of communism, fascism and democracy have shaped all of our lives and still play a huge part in how the world is run. Thus, Russia and Eastern Europe were communist until 1990, China has a communist government and many of the regimes of South America and Africa are fascist military dictatorships. In Western Europe, the USA and Israel the governments are democracies.

We can study the Era of the Second World War as a fight between communism, fascism and democracy, with a fourth idea, nationalism, having a big say in what has gone on. You can jot down on paper what you think communism, fascism, democracy and nationalism mean, a sentence for each, and then discuss them.

To help you come to grips with communism, fascism and democracy I put in **A** and worked out chart **B**.

B	Democratic	Fascist	Communist
All adults have the vote	No elections	No elections
Lots of political parties	One political party	One political party to represent the working class
Tolerates all parties	Hates communists	Hates fascists
Believes in using argument to solve problems	Happy to beat up and kill enemies	Happy to beat up and kill enemies
Parties should have no private armies	Party can have a private army of thugs	Party can have a private army of thugs
No party uniform	Party uniform, flag and emblem	Party uniform, flag and emblem
Backs private enterprise	Backs private enterprise	State owns all banks, factories, farms, shops, etc.
Free speech and media - e.g. press, radio, TV,	No free speech, state controls media	No free speech, state controls media
No army power	Army backs government	Army backs government
Freedom of worship	State controls the church	No religion - only communism allowed
No secret police	Secret police	Secret police
No political prisoners	State enemies jailed	State enemies jailed
Tolerance of Jews	Jews lose all rights	Tolerance of Jews (in theory)
Believes in working with other countries to solve problems	Fiercely nationalist	Believes in world revolution to spread communism; you support revolutionary groups in other countries to bring about a revolution

Communist hammer and sickle

Nazi swastika

Italian fasces

Activity (AT1)

Spider diagrams are a great way of getting across ideas. You can create your own history diagram on communism, fascism and democracy.

a Take one of these ideas, and make out a diagram to show what the word means. You can put the word at the centre of the page, and use a spider diagram with pictures and words to get the ideas across.

b Design and include your own symbol for communism, fascism or democracy.

c Hold a class display of your diagrams and symbols.

ACTIVITY · ACTIVITY

Hitler's Plans for Europe

'Hitler, he caused the Second World War' said my taxi driver. Did he?

Adolf Hitler became ruler of Germany in 1933. Six years later Germany invaded Poland and the Second World War had begun.

What did Hitler want? I took **A** from Hitler's book *Mein Kampf* (My Struggle). *Mein Kampf* became the Nazi bible. Hitler did much of what it said after 1933. In *Mein Kampf* Hitler claimed the Germans were members of a master race, the Aryans. He said that the Aryans would get rid of the Jews and conquer other lesser races such as the Slavs, i.e. people like the Poles and Russians. *Mein Kampf* stated what this meant for Europe:

The frontiers of 1914 mean nothing in respect of Germany's future… There can only be sense in it [a treaty with France] if it offers backing for the space [Lebensraum = room to live] which our people need in Europe. For gaining colonies will not solve that question - nothing will, in fact, but gaining land to settle [in Europe, which means]… we will turn our eyes eastwards. We have ended our pre-war plans of gaining colonies and trade. We are going over to the land policy of the future [in Eastern Europe]. **(A)**

(adapted from A. Hitler, *Mein Kampf*, 1924)

1. We demand the union of all Germans to form a Greater Germany on the basis of the right of the self-determination enjoyed by nations.
2. We demand equal rights for the German People in its dealings with other nations, and abolition of the Peace Treaties of Versailles…
3. We demand land and territory for the keeping of our people and for the settlement of superfluous [more than needed] population. **(B)**

(extracts from the 1920 Nazi Party Programme, adapted from A. Hitler, *Mein Kampf*, 1924)

FACTFILE

1933 Hitler leaves the League of Nations, the body set up to keep world peace after 1918.
1934 Hitler tries to unite Germany and Austria, the Anschluss.
1935 Germany builds up armed forces. Conscription starts.

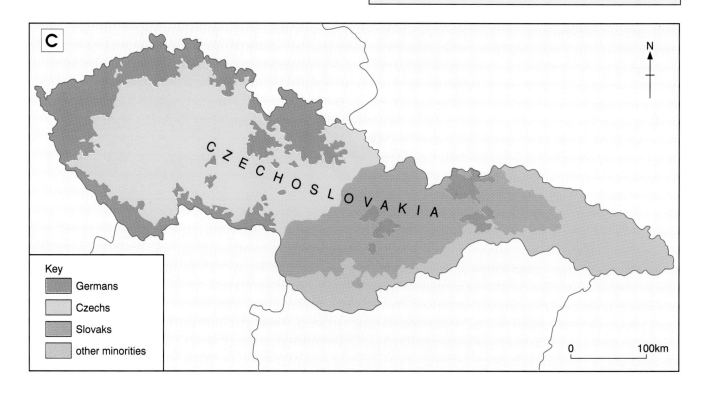

C

CZECHOSLOVAKIA

N

Key
- Germans
- Czechs
- Slovaks
- other minorities

0   100km

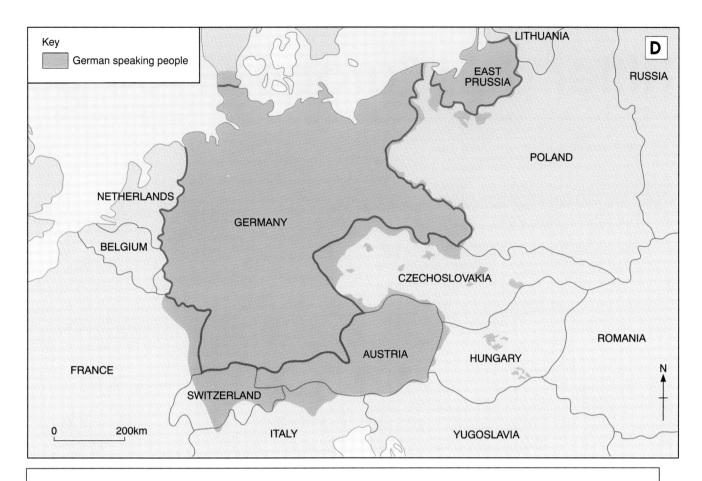

Key
German speaking people

LITHUANIA

D

EAST PRUSSIA

RUSSIA

POLAND

NETHERLANDS

GERMANY

BELGIUM

CZECHOSLOVAKIA

FRANCE

AUSTRIA

HUNGARY

ROMANIA

SWITZERLAND

N

0   200km

ITALY

YUGOSLAVIA

History Detective!

As a young historian you can use your skills to try and work out from sources **A-D** and map **B** on page 18 what Hitler might do in the 1930s. You can do this as an adviser to either the British or Hitler's German government in 1934.

1 Working on the sources (AT3, AT2)
First, to help get your facts straight, work through these questions. Give reasons for your answers where you can.

a Find East Prussia, Poland, Czechoslovakia, Austria, Hungary and Russia on the map on page 18.
b Study **A** and **B**. Do they suggest:
• that Germany will want back all the lands in Europe and abroad it lost in 1918?
• why Hitler would sign a treaty with France?

• where German settlers would live?
• who might be citizens of the new Greater Germany?
• who wouldn't be?
• what might happen to them?
• what Hitler would do to the Versailles settlement?
• how useful *Mein Kampf* is as a source for what Hitler thinks?
c Study **B** and **D** to say which countries Hitler would have to invade or to have treaties with to make sure that all Germans lived in Germany.
d What does **B** suggest that Hitler might do to Czechoslovakia if Germany conquered it.
e **C** and **D** are based on German maps of the Hitler era. In what ways might they mislead? What is their value to you as a young historian?

2 Hitler's plans (AT2, AT1)
You can now work out a plan of what Hitler might do in 1934, *either* from a British *or*

from a German viewpoint.
a Your plan should look at these points which are listed in alphabetical order: Austria; Czechoslovakia as a country; France; Germans in Czechoslovakia; Germans and a Greater Germany; Poland, the Polish corridor and East Prussia; Russia and Communism.
If you work in groups or as a class you can split the countries up among you.
b When you have ideas about each country, work out a **Hitler Plan** for the whole of Europe.

3 Report back (AT1)
You can explain your plan to the class. The class can then discuss different plans, which seem most likely and why they differ.

ACTIVITY · ACTIVITY

Hitler and Europe, 1934-38

'We Germans should be one race' said Fritz. For two years, since 1934, he had been a member of the Hitler Youth. Fritz went on, 'When our brave leader Adolf Hitler tried to join Germany and Austria together in 1934 it was the right thing to do. After all, he was an Austrian, and the people of Austria are as German as I. Why shouldn't we be one country? If it was okay for new countries to be set up after 1918 along the lines of their races, why shouldn't Germans be treated the same way? The only reason Hitler wasn't able to merge us with Austria was because the ruler of Italy, Mussolini, wouldn't have it. He was afraid that we might march our armies over the Alps and conquer Italy, just like we did in the past! We Germans have changed, all we want is peace and friendship, and to live together as one big, happy German family. Yet you talk all the time as if we are the same kind of people as in 1914.'

A Nazi soldier stands guard outside a closed Jewish shop.

Well, I said, what about the way Hitler has treated the Jews, the communists, the trade unionists and the other political parties? They have all been flung into jail or killed, and there is now no freedom in Germany (see **A**). At this Fritz thumped the table and shouted, 'traitors, murderers, revolutionaries - you know they burnt down our parliament building in 1934. If Hitler's storm troopers hadn't swept up this scum they would have wrecked the country. Look at how Germany is peace and quiet at the moment, and getting richer all the time.'

Stepping stones to glory.

German rearmament and her march into the Rhineland led Lowe to show Hitler marching across the backs of democracies like Britain and France. Find out where Danzig is, and what point the cartoon is making here.

Maybe Fritz had a point, but then I said to him, 'How can you back your government's marching of troops into the Rhineland in 1936?' He thought for a second and said, 'The Rhineland is part of Germany, it always has been. After the First World War we were forced to sign the Versailles peace treaty which kept our troops out of the Rhineland. And we know how the French behaved when they sent their forces into the Rhineland in 1923 to grab coal, claiming that we owed them money. Hitler was right to march our troops back into the Rhineland, after all it is Germany. Now that we have got the bridges over the Rhine back into our hands we are safe from attack from the West (**B**). Hitler can feel free to win back our lost lands in Austria,

Czechoslovakia and Poland.' My blood ran cold at these words, for Fritz seemed to be saying that Germany was getting ready for war.

If Hitler tried to conquer these countries Britain and France would have to fight to save them. When I put these points to him he paused and said, 'They will never fight for Czechs and Poles. Your leaders know that we have got right on our side. The Germans in Eastern Europe should all belong to a Greater Germany. These small countries will survive without the Germans in them. We will make sure they live on.'

He went on, 'And what about Russia. Those communist swine are trying to conquer the world. If Germany does not become strong and stand up to the Red Army, Eastern Europe will fall into Russia's hands. Then see where you are! Communism will soon try to spread to France, Britain and America. You can be safe in our hands. With our good friends the Japanese we will keep the red bear in its cage and make sure that it is a threat to no one. Look at how our brave soldiers are fighting against the red menace in Spain at the moment.' Fritz was talking about the Spanish Civil War in which German and Italian forces were fighting for the fascist General Franco against the democratic government whose ally was Russia. The British Government refused to take sides, although it was secretly backing the fascists.

To me the world seemed in great danger. The Germans and Italians were drawing closer and closer together, for Germany had also backed the Italians taking of Abyssinia (modern Ethiopia) in 1935-36. In the Far East the Japanese had attacked China, and the Japanese army was on the war path. Germany and Italy had signed a treaty to help each other. Britain did nothing to stop Italy's leader, Mussolini (C).

HE TOOK WATER AND WASHED HIS HANDS

Mussolini is dressed as a Roman emperor. He is standing over the British foreign secretary, who is washing his hands, to show that Spain and Abyssinia are not his concern.

Points of View

The interview with Fritz and cartoons **B** and **C** put across a point of view.

1 Studying the text and sources (AT3, AT1)
a Read the text slowly. What does Fritz tell you about:
- Germany's point of view in 1934
- why Germany marched into the Rhineland
- his thoughts about Czechoslovakia and Poland
- his views on Italy and Abyssinia
- his view of communist Russia

b How would you rewrite Fritz's story from the viewpoint of a British pupil of the same age who felt that Germany should be stood up to.

2 Cartoon captions (AT2)
For each cartoon (**B** and **C**) produce:
- a title for an anti Nazi British newspaper
- a title for a Nazi German newspaper
- a British account of what the cartoon is showing
- a German account of what the cartoon is showing

3 History cartoon (AT1)
a Draw your own history cartoon for 1936 showing the dangers to world peace. Refer to:
- the Spanish Civil War
- Russia
- Abyssinia
- Eastern Europe

b Add a caption to your cartoon to explain what it shows.

Steps to War, 1938-39

Newspaper headlines always trumpet the big story of the day. In **March 1938** many headlines were about how Germany had swallowed up Austria. We call the union of Germany and Austria the Anschluss.

From **April 1938** onwards lots of newspaper stories were about Czechoslovakia **(A)**, a country which was in danger of attack from Germany.

• Hitler demanded that all Germans should live in a German state. The problem was that there were about three million Germans living in part of Czechoslovakia called the Sudetenland **(A)**.
• Hitler claimed that the Sudetenland should be part of Germany.
• Czechoslovakia had been set up as a country as part of the peace settlement after the First World War.
• Britain and France had said that they would protect Czechoslovakia from attack.

By **July 1938** Europe was on the brink of war. The British prime minister, Neville Chamberlain, had been pushing a policy of **appeasement**, or peace at any price. Appeasement meant giving in to the demands of Hitler.

Throughout the summer of 1938 the leaders of Europe tried to solve the Czechoslovakian crisis. They put forward plans to carve up Czechoslovakia in a number of ways. Hitler claimed huge chunks of the country; Britain and France said that he should get less.

It seemed that war might break out at any time. In **September 1938**

• Hitler called a meeting of Europe's leaders in Munich to try and sort out the mess.
• Chamberlain flew to Munich where he met Hitler of Germany, Mussolini of Italy and France's leader.
• The leaders drew up a plan which gave Hitler what he wanted, the Munich Agreement.
• The Czechs were not asked what they thought.

Chamberlain **(B)** flew home to great praise. Hitler's troops marched into the Sudetenland.

The Munich agreement did not last long (see *Factfile*).

FACTFILE

March 1939
Germany conquered rest of Czechoslovakia. Hitler gained all of Czechoslovakia's guns and planes, and the huge Skoda arms factory. Czechoslovakia lost land to Hungary. A Slovak state was set up under German control.
Hitler seized the city of Memel in Lithuania. England, France, Italy and Japan had guaranteed its independence at Versailles.
April
Hitler now turned to Poland. The war clouds gathered. Hitler claimed that Germany should get back the lands it lost to Poland after the First World War. This would mean that
• the city of Danzig would become German again
• Poland could use Danzig as a free port
• a rail and road corridor through Germany would link Danzig and Poland
• Poland's borders would be recognised as permanent
• Poland and Germany would sign a 25-year peace treaty
Mussolini invaded and conquered Albania despite British protests.
Britain introduced conscription – military service for all fit men over 20.
May
Italy and Germany signed a military and political treaty – the Pact of Steel.
June–July
Britain got ready to fight. Hitler took steps to seize Danzig and set up an armed force in the city.
September 1939 war broke out.
• Germany invaded Poland.
• Poland refused to surrender.
• Britain and France declared war on Germany.
• Germany and Russia had signed a peace treaty.
• After the defeat of the Polish army the Russians and Germans split up Poland between them.

Steps to War

It is August 1939. Europe is on the brink of war. Work on your own, in pairs or in groups of three or four. Each person or group represents one of the following powers:
• Britain
• Poland
• France
• Russia
• Germany
• Italy

1 Review (AT1, AT2)
a Work out newspaper headlines for the main events of 1938 and 1939 (see text and the *Factfile*) from the viewpoint of the power you are representing.
b For **B** say what headlines and caption the following papers might give the picture: a German (pro Nazi), British (pro government) and Czechoslovakian (anti German).

2 Messages (AT2, AT1)
You have to send messages and negotiate with the other five powers, or just work out the messages each power might send.
a Each group or individual representing one power agrees on the messages it will send to each of the other powers. The messages will be about making alliances and how you will treat that power and the other countries.
b Work out five messages in all. Include whom they are from, whom they are to and the date.
c Send your messages.

3 Responding (AT2)
a When a message arrives discuss it.
b Work out your plans for your country in the light of all the messages you have had, and what you feel about them.
c Write a reply to each of the other five powers.

4 Summing up (AT1)
a Work out the position which your country has.
b Discuss why you think war broke out in September 1939, i.e. what were its causes.
c Write an essay on **The Causes of World War II**.

ACTIVITY · ACTIVITY

Spread of the Second World War

From 1939-45 war tore Europe apart. New struggles broke out all the time. The war spread through **nine stages**. The maps and captions deal with the nine stages. The **cause cards** list causes for the spread of the war. You have to match each card to its right stage.

Stage 1 On 1 September 1939 Germany attacked Poland. Russia occupied Eastern Poland at the same time, having allied with Germany, **A**.

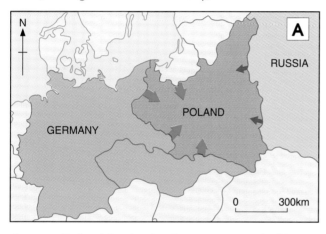

Stage 2 Poland fought the Germans instead of surrendering.
Stage 3 On 3 September 1939 Britain and France declared war on Germany.
Stage 4 On 9 April 1940 Germany invaded Denmark and Norway.
Stage 5 On 10 May 1940 Germany invaded Belgium, the Netherlands, Luxemburg and France, **B**.

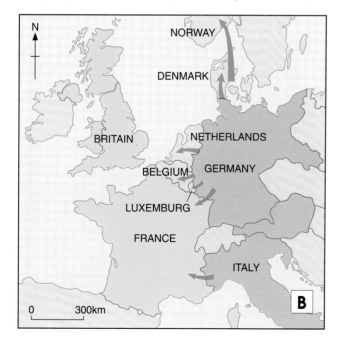

Stage 6 10 June 1940 Italy declared war on Britain and France.
Stage 7 Autumn 1940-Spring 1941 Bulgaria, Hungary and Romania became allies of Germany.
Stage 8 Germany and Italy invaded Greece and Yugoslavia in Autumn 1940-Spring 1941, **C**.
Stage 9 Germany invaded Russia, Operation Barbarossa, 22 June 1941, **D**.

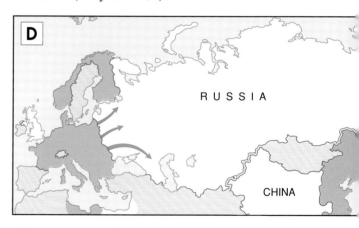

Cause cards

Each cause card gives **one** reason why war broke out in one of the **nine stages**. Match each cause card to its right **stage**.

Card 1 Germany wanted Norwegian high quality steel for making weapons.
Card 2 Mussolini, Italy's leader, wanted to share in the glory of beating France.

Card 3 Hitler thought that the Russian people were sub-human and should become the slaves of the Germans.

Card 4 Germany claimed she should have back the Polish corridor. Most of the people living there were Germans. The peace settlement of 1918 had said that race should be the main reason for drawing a country's boundaries.

Card 5 Hitler said that German people should settle in Russia and take over Russian land and resources - *Lebensraum*.

Card 6 Bulgaria, Hungary and Romania had no choice - Germany could have overrun them if she had wanted to.

Card 7 Britain and France had promised that they would fight on Poland's side if Germany attacked her.

Card 8 Britain and France kept their promise to fight on Poland's side if the Germans attacked her. They refused to make peace even though they could not send troops to Poland nor attack Germany in the West.

Card 9 Britain and France thought that this was the last chance to stop Germany from taking over the whole of Europe.

Card 10 Hitler's breaking of his promise to Czechoslovakia in 1939 meant that he could not be trusted and that the British and French would have to fight him. If not, he would conquer all of Europe.

Card 11 Bulgaria, Hungary and Romania wanted to be on the winning side.

Card 12 Poland said she would fight to keep the Polish corridor. It was her only outlet to the sea; without it she would be ruined.

Card 13 In Russia Germany could expect a rising of peasants and workers who were suffering under communism and of nationalities which wanted to win their freedom.

Card 14 Hitler thought no one would stop him from seizing Poland. He had got his own way without a fight before, the last time being when Germany had swallowed up most of Czechoslovakia in 1938-39.

Card 15 Greece was stopping Italy from taking over the Eastern Mediterranean.

Card 16 Germany would find it much easier to fight France and Britain if it took over small neutral powers like Holland, Belgium, Luxemburg.

Card 17 Poland could not fight against the might of Germany and Russia. She would give in without going to war, and this would mean that Britain and France would not come to her help.

Card 18 Greece was a likely ally of England against Germany and Italy.

Card 19 Italy could seize lands it had always claimed from France.

Card 20 Bulgaria, Hungary and Romania had governments like Germany's, and it made sense to become a German ally.

Card 21 Yugoslavia could be split up among the Bulgarians, Hungarians and Romanians.

Card 22 Poles always fought Germans and Russians when they tried to crush her. As late as 1920 Poles had fought off a Russian attack.

Card 23 Hitler had a deep seated hatred of Russian communism.

Card 24 Yugoslavia was supporting the Allies against Germany and might even join the war against her.

Card 25 The Russian armed forces were weak after Stalin, Russia's communist ruler, had killed most of its officers in the 1930s. The Red Army had done badly when it had invaded Finland in 1940.

Card 26 Bulgaria, Hungary and Romania could grab lands they had claimed in the past.

Card 27 Mussolini, Italy's leader, was Hitler's friend and ally. It made sense to join in on the winning side.

Causes of World War II

A **cause** is a reason for something happening. You can use the **cause cards** to think about the causes of each **stage** in the spread of World War II in Europe.

1 Reading and research (AT3)
Find out what you can about why war broke out in 1939 and spread through Europe from 1939-41.

2 Timeline/map work (AT1)
a Make out a timeline for the spread of war, or mark on an outline map of Europe how the war spread.
b For a class timeline you could split the stages up between you and draw a diagram or picture to show what happened for your stage.

3 Sorting the cards (AT1)
a Make or write out a heading for each of the nine stages.
b Sort the 27 cause cards under their right headings.
c For each stage put the cause cards into what you think are their order of importance.
d You can compare your order for each stage with that of your partner or the rest of the class.
e In cartoon or diagram form, show how the war spread in the four stages shown on maps **A-D**, *or* write an account of how and why war spread from 1939-41.

ACTIVITY · ACTIVITY

The Second World War in Europe

Who fought whom in the Second World War in Europe (map **A**)?

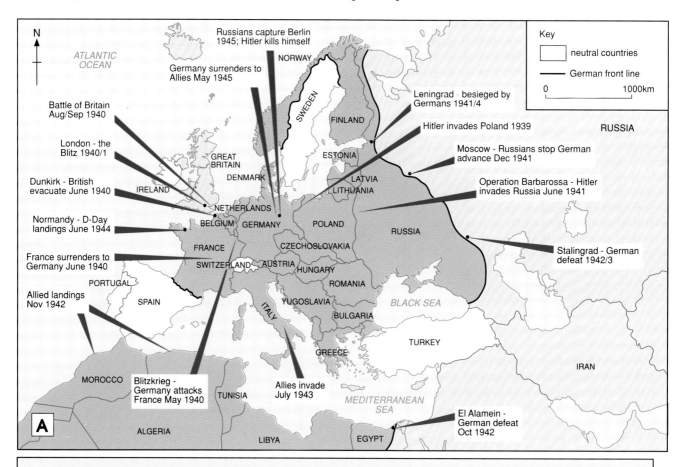

Russians capture Berlin 1945; Hitler kills himself

Germany surrenders to Allies May 1945

Battle of Britain Aug/Sep 1940

London - the Blitz 1940/1

Dunkirk - British evacuate June 1940

Normandy - D-Day landings June 1944

France surrenders to Germany June 1940

Allied landings Nov 1942

Leningrad - besieged by Germans 1941/4

Hitler invades Poland 1939

Moscow - Russians stop German advance Dec 1941

Operation Barbarossa - Hitler invades Russia June 1941

Stalingrad - German defeat 1942/3

Blitzkrieg - Germany attacks France May 1940

Allies invade July 1943

El Alamein - German defeat Oct 1942

Key
neutral countries
German front line
0   1000km

ATLANTIC OCEAN, NORWAY, SWEDEN, FINLAND, ESTONIA, LATVIA, LITHUANIA, GREAT BRITAIN, IRELAND, DENMARK, NETHERLANDS, BELGIUM, GERMANY, POLAND, RUSSIA, FRANCE, CZECHOSLOVAKIA, SWITZERLAND, AUSTRIA, HUNGARY, ROMANIA, PORTUGAL, SPAIN, YUGOSLAVIA, BULGARIA, ITALY, GREECE, BLACK SEA, TURKEY, IRAN, MOROCCO, TUNISIA, MEDITERRANEAN SEA, EGYPT, ALGERIA, LIBYA, RUSSIA

A

Mapwork and a Timeline

On your own, in pairs, threes, groups or as a form you can create a **map** and a **timeline** to see the impact of the Second World War on Europe.

1 Year maps (AT1)
a Using **A**, try quickly drawing two sketch maps of Europe, one for 1941 and the other for 1945, to show who was on whose side. See how your ideas match the countries shown in the list!
b For each year of the war produce a map which shows how the war is going. You can do this as a cut out or overlay of the area which Germany and Italy ruled. Use four colours or shadings for:

- German and Italian rule
- German allies
- Britain and Allies
- neutrals

2 Timeline (AT3, AT1)
a Make out a timeline in your book for the key events in the Second World War in Europe shown on the back cover.
b Take **one** key event, and design a sheet to put up or hang on a class timeline for the war.
c Research the event, putting down the main facts on your sheet.
d You can include a picture, map or written account.
e Tell the class about your sheet.

ACTIVITY · ACTIVITY

The Fortunes of War, 1939-45				
	German and Italian rule	German Allies	Britain and Allies	Neutrals
1939 Sep	Germany Italy Libya Albania Poland	Slovakia Bulgaria Hungary Romania	Britain France	Russia (incl. E. Poland Latvia, Lithuania, Estonia) Greece Turkey Sweden Switzerland Yugoslavia Greece
1940 Dec	Germany Italy Albania Poland Holland Belgium France Norway Morocco Algeria Denmark Greece Libya Yugoslavia	Slovakia Bulgaria Hungary Romania	Britain	Russia Turkey Sweden Switzerland
1941 Dec	Germany Italy Albania Poland Holland Belgium France Norway Morocco Algeria Denmark Greece Libya Yugoslavia	Slovakia Bulgaria Hungary Romania	Britain Russia USA	Turkey Sweden Switzerland
1942 Dec	Germany Italy Albania Poland Holland Belgium France Norway Denmark Greece Yugoslavia	Slovakia Bulgaria Hungary Romania	Britain Russia Algeria Morocco Libya USA	Turkey Sweden Switzerland
1943 Dec	Germany Italy France Norway Holland Belgium Denmark Greece Yugoslavia Albania		Britain Russia Morocco Algeria Bulgaria Romania Hungary Slovakia Libya USA	Turkey Sweden Switzerland
1944 Dec	Germany Norway Denmark		Britain Russia Morocco Algeria Holland Belgium France Greece Italy Yugoslavia Bulgaria Romania Hungary Slovakia Libya Albania USA	Turkey Sweden Switzerland
1945 June	Germany		Britain Russia Morocco Algeria Holland Belgium France Greece Italy Yugoslavia Denmark Norway Bulgaria Romania Hungary Czechoslovakia USA	Turkey Sweden Switzerland

Churchill, Roosevelt and Stalin

Churchill, Roosevelt and Stalin were the wartime leaders of Britain, America and Russia. Sources **A-F** are about them.

Churchill, Sir Winston (1874-1965)

66 *Winston Leonard Spencer Churchill was the grandson of the Duke of Marlborough. ... Before and during World War I he served as head of the Admiralty, and then resigned from government to command troops in France for a time. He was Chancellor of the Exchequer from 1924 to 1929.*

During the 1930s Churchill was not a government minister. He warned that there was a danger of another world war, but many people ignored him. However, when World War II came the prime minister, Neville Chamberlain, put him in charge of the Admiralty once again. And when German armies were overrunning Europe in May 1940, King George VI asked him to be prime minister and lead a coalition government of all parties. His courage and his speeches inspired the people to withstand air raids and military defeats, and carry on to victory. 99 **(B)**

(*Oxford Children's Encyclopedia*, Volume 5, 1991)

Roosevelt, Franklin Delano (1882-1945)

66 *Franklin D. Roosevelt had to fight hard to overcome a physical handicap. He developed polio at the age of 40, and his legs were paralysed.*

In 1928 he was elected Governor of New York State, and four years later became President of the USA.

The country was in a terrible state. One worker in four was out of work, and many families were too poor even to buy food. Five thousand banks had failed. Roosevelt promised a New Deal, and told Americans: 'The only thing we have to fear is fear itself.' He launched a programme to put the country back on its feet. ...

In 1940, with World War II raging in Europe, Roosevelt was elected for a third term, the first and last president to be so. In December 1941 the USA entered the war. Roosevelt guided the country through its darkest days, working closely with the leaders of Britain and the Soviet Union, Winston Churchill and Joseph Stalin. He won a fourth election in 1944, but in April 1945, with war victory in sight, he died suddenly. 99 **(D)**

(*Oxford Children's Encyclopedia*, Volume 6, 1991)

E

Stalin, Joseph (1879-1953)

> *Joseph Vissarionovich Dzhugashvili was born in the hillside village of Gori in Georgia. His father, who died when he was 11, was a shoemaker and his mother a washerwoman. He joined the Russian Social-Democratic Workers' Party and became a full-time revolutionary. His bank raids and other daring escapades often landed him in prison or exile, but he always managed to escape from his place of exile. He proved himself to be tough, brave and dedicated, and was invited by Lenin to join the Bolshevik Party leadership in 1912. It was then that he took the name 'Stalin' (man of steel).*
>
> *In 1917, Stalin was a loyal supporter of Lenin's seizure of power. In 1922, he became secretary of the Communist Party (as the Bolsheviks were now known). Lenin died in 1924.*
>
> *In the years that followed, Stalin helped to build a strong nation through a series of Five-Year Plans intended to industrialize and modernize Soviet Russia. His greatest achievement was to lead his country, as 'Generalissimo', to victory over the Nazis in World War II. After this, communist influence spread through much of Europe.* (F)

(*Oxford Children's Encyclopedia*, Volume 6, 1991)

Obituary or Stamp

August 1945, Europe lay in ruins. Germany's leader, Hitler, trapped in his Berlin bunker, had killed himself. If the Allies had lost the war the Germans may have shot Churchill, Roosevelt and Stalin. When a famous person dies newspapers print the story of his or her life, an obituary. You can produce an obituary, 1-4, or design stamps, 5.

1 Planning (AT1)
Prepare an obituary of under 100 words for one or more of Churchill, Roosevelt or Stalin. In groups of three or more split the leaders up among you so that you write about them all.

2 Research (AT3)
a Study the sources. Pick out the key facts in the career of the leader you have chosen, and say what ideas about him his picture gives.
b Find out from other sources what you can about your chosen leader: his character, his ideas, his plans. Choose any sources you would like to include in your obituary.

3 Writing the obituary (AT2, AT1)
a Design the obituary with a title, a picture and its caption and an account of the leader's role in the war.
b Write the obituary from the viewpoint of either an American, British, German or Russian government newspaper in June 1945.
c How might such obituaries have been different in 1941 or 1951?

4 Judgment (AT1, AT2)
Display the obituaries, and judge which is best in covering all the main points of the leader's wartime career, or take turns to answer questions about the leader whose obituary you have written.

5 Stamp design (AT2, AT1)
As an alternative activity you can design an official stamp for America, Britain and Russia for 1945 showing their leaders. As a 100-word leaflet used to sell each stamp, put down the ideas you would like it to get across. To help you, work through 2 above.

ACTIVITY · ACTIVITY ·

The Conquest of France

In 1939 most German, Polish, British and French soldiers moved at the speed of a walking horse. Germany had a small force of planes and tanks and 4500 parachute troops. This force fought in a new way - **blitzkrieg**, which in German means 'lightning war'. Blitzkrieg changed the history of the world.

What was blitzkrieg? I picked **A** from what Britain's greatest expert on warfare wrote:

❝ *Guderian [a German general] has related [told] how, before the war, his imagination was fired by the idea of deep strategic penetration by independent armoured forces - a long-range tank drive to cut the main arteries of the opposing army far back behind its front.* ❞ **(A)**

(B.H. Liddell Hart, *History of the Second World War*, Pan, 1956)

Blitzkrieg **(B)** saw ground troops using tanks, motorbikes and lorries (with the support of dive bombers and parachute troops) to cut off a much bigger enemy army. In May 1940 the Germans used blitzkrieg to conquer France.

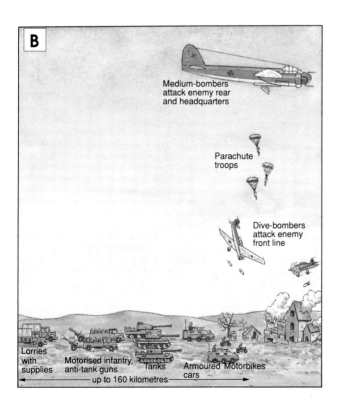

B

Medium-bombers attack enemy rear and headquarters

Parachute troops

Dive-bombers attack enemy front line

Lorries with supplies — Motorised infantry, anti-tank guns — Tanks — Armoured cars — Motorbikes

— up to 160 kilometres —

A.J.P. Taylor, a famous historian, tells us of the impact of blitzkrieg in May 1940:

❝ *The Belgians relied on their great fortress at Ebene Emael. German pioneers took it by the simple expedient [trick] of landing from gliders on its roof and thrusting explosives through the air shafts. On 12 May the Belgians abandoned the line of the Meuse. Two days later British and French forces made contact with the Belgians and began to coordinate their defence. On 15 May the Allies had a more pressing concern: not how to defend Belgium, but how to get out of it. The Germans had broken through further south on the Meuse at Sedan. The entire active force of the Allies was in danger of being cut off... The German and French General Staffs had calculated that it would take nine days for the Germans to reach the Meuse. Guderian said four. He reached it in two... At 1500 hours on 13 May, the first German soldiers crossed the Meuse. French resistance was feeble. German tanks crossed at dawn the next day, and by 15 May Guderian's way was clear. He swept forward, disregarding orders to halt*

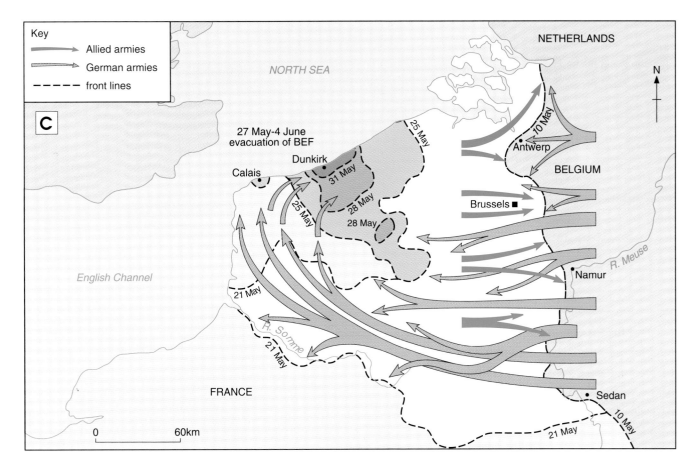

Key

→ Allied armies
⇒ German armies
– – – front lines

C

NORTH SEA

27 May-4 June
evacuation of BEF

Dunkirk

Calais

31 May

25 May

28 May

28 May

English Channel

21 May

R. Somme

21 May

FRANCE

0   60km

NETHERLANDS

N

10 May

Antwerp

BELGIUM

Brussels ■

R. Meuse

Namur

Sedan

10 May

21 May

---

from his army commander... The German tanks drive unimpeded along the open roads. When they ran out of petrol, the crews stopped at the nearest pump, filled up without paying and drove on. Occasionally they stopped to milk a cow. 🙶🙶 **(D)**

(A.J.P. Taylor, *The Second World War*, Hamish Hamilton/Rainbird, 1975)

By the end of May the French and British had been beaten. The British army was trapped on the French coast at Dunkirk. It seemed doomed.

Map Work

Produce a map for a school textbook with all the facts and ideas you need to know about how the Germans used blitzkrieg to beat France in May 1914.

The map (AT1, AT3)
a You can use drawings or pictures to illustrate your points.
b On a copy of the outline of **C** mark what happened on: 10, 12, 14, 15 May and at the frontline on 21, 25, 28 and 31 May.
c Give your map a title.
d Write a five-line caption saying what blitzkrieg was; when and where it had been used before 1940; what success it had had.
e Include with your map how you would attack the small town on **E** with the units shown in the key.

E

0   1km

a

b

c

Key
a village - enemy force dug in in trenches with machine guns and artillery
b small town - enemy troops with ten tanks
c farmhouse - enemy dug in around it with a small force of machine guns

German forces
reconnaisance units on motorbikes
squadron of bomber planes
tank force - 50 tanks
towed artillery
infantry on motorbikes and in lorries
infantrymen with flame throwers

The Germans are advancing from the South.

ACTIVITY · ACTIVITY ·

Dunkirk

Do you know any old person who might be able to tell you something about Dunkirk (see the *Factfile*)? I chose **A** and **B** to give you two views of Dunkirk. Spike Milligan, who kept a diary of his time as a private in the army in the war, tells us in **A** of the impact that Dunkirk made on him. **B** is an official British painting of the Dunkirk beach at the time boats from England were rescuing British and French troops.

66 *Dunkirk*

The first eventful date in my army career was the eve of the final evacuation from Dunkirk, when I was sent to the O.P. [Observation Post] at Galley Hill to help the cook. I had only been in the Army twenty-four hours when it happened. Each news bulletin from BBC told an increasingly depressing story. Things were indeed very grave. For days previously we could hear the distant sound of explosions and heavy gunfire from across the Channel. Sitting in a crude wood O.P. heaped with earth at two in the morning with a Ross Rifle with only five rounds made you feel so bloody useless in relation to what was going on the other side. Five rounds of ammo, and that was between the whole O.P. The day of the actual Dunkirk evacuation the Channel was like a piece of polished steel. I'd never seen a sea so calm. One would say it was miraculous. I presume that something like this had happened to create the 'Angel of Mons' legend. That afternoon Bombardier Andrews and I went down for a swim. It would appear we were the only two people on the south coast having one. With the distant booms, the still sea, and just two figures on the landscape, it all seemed very very strange. We swam in silence. Occasionally, a squadron of Spitfires or Hurricanes headed out towards France. I remember so clearly, Bombardier Andrews standing up in the water, putting his hands on his hips, and gazing towards where the B.E.F. was fighting for its life. It was the first time I'd seen genuine concern on a British soldier's face; 'I can't see how they're going to get 'em out,' he said. We sat in the warm water for a while. We felt so helpless. Next day the news of the 'small armada' came through on the afternoon news. As the immensity of the defeat became apparent, somehow the evacuation turned it into a strange victory. I don't think the nation ever reached such a feeling of solidarity as in that week at any other time during the war. 99 **(A)**

(Spike Milligan, *Adolf Hitler, My Part in his Downfall*, Penguin, 1972)

B

24 May 1940 German attack had cut off Allied armies in the North of France and Belgium. British army retreats to Dunkirk.

27 May Belgium surrenders.
• Gort, commander of the British Expeditionary Force (BEF), decides to save his army.
• Evacuation of British and French troops begins from Dunkirk. British fighter planes keep Germans at bay, 860 small boats, fishing vessels, pleasure boats, ferries help bring off British and French troops. Destroyers carry most of the men.
• All guns and equipment left behind except for the Guards who came back with their rifles and kit.

4 June Evacuation completed of 200,000 British and 140,000 French troops who were brought back safely to England.

Dunkirk!

What did Dunkirk mean? Why do we still talk about it? We can get an idea from looking at it from the viewpoints of people involved. We can use these to create an historical collage of *ideas* and *views* in your books or on a poster. You can work on your own or in pairs, threes or groups to plan the work, split up jobs among you and produce your finished work.

1 Finding out - studying the sources (AT3)
a Think of questions you can ask old people about Dunkirk, such as how they heard about it, what they were doing, and their feelings, thoughts and fears at the time.
b Using your questions, make out an interview form and interview old people you know about Dunkirk.
c Collect and pool the class's interviews about Dunkirk.
d Read **A** quickly.

• Jot down a word or phrase which sums up his ideas. Pool these.
• Then pick out from **A** the sentences which support the key ideas you have come up with.

e In **B** what does the picture suggest about how the British and French were evacuated.
f Study **B**.

• What single thought do you think the artist wants you to have about Dunkirk?
• Study either the beach, the sea, the sky or the clouds of smoke and pick out one thing which gives an idea of what was going on.

g Read **A**. How does it support or oppose the ideas about Dunkirk given in **B**?

h Find out what else you can about Dunkirk, and copy or collect pictures and accounts of it.

2 Viewpoints (AT2)
a Identify with *either* one figure in **B** *or* a German, *or* the person Spike Milligan mentions *or* one of the people you have interviewed.
b Work out an account of Dunkirk from his or her viewpoint. Mention:

• the German attack on France
• the way the campaign went for the BEF, the BEF's role
• the British and French encircled
• the German attacks on the beach
• the armada of boats and the role of the navy
• the return to England

c On your collage put what you think were

• the causes of Dunkirk
• the consequences of Dunkirk
• why it is part of our national heritage

d Think of a caption for picture **B** from either a British, a French or a German point of view.

3 The collage (AT2, AT1)
a Think of a title.
b Work out your design.
c Write captions for the items you include.
d Display your work, and each person or group can tell the class what their collage shows.

ACTIVITY · ACTIVITY

Occupation

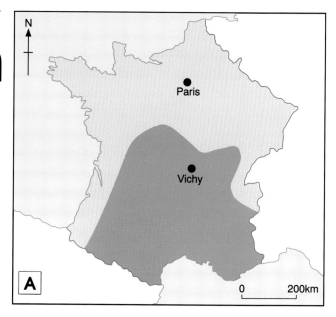

What was it like to live in a country which the Germans had occupied? In France the Germans took over the North of the country, in the South a French government was set up at Vichy under German control (see **A**).

Networks of resistance fighters, the Maquis, carried on the struggle against the Germans (see *Factfile*).

FACTFILE

- There were strict laws and rules about where you could live, work and pass your spare time, and a curfew.
- Identity papers had to be carried at all times.
- Spot checks were common.
- Most French lived quiet, normal lives from 1940-45, but many joined the French Resistance.
- Between 1940-45 the Germans tortured and killed some 60,000 French resisters.
- Around 200,000 members of the Resistance were deported from France to labour and concentration camps. Only about 50,000 came back alive.
- The German secret police or Gestapo carried out a full-time campaign against the Resistance.
- Thousands of French informers and spies helped the Gestapo.
- The French lived in a world of fear, hatred, suspicion and doubt.

What was it like to belong to the Resistance? Brigitte Friang was a student in Paris. She gave up her studies and worked for the Resistance instead.

❝ *By November 1943 I had decided that it was too dangerous to live at home. There was a curfew in Paris and you couldn't be in the streets between midnight and five o'clock in the morning... I had to go to the countryside one weekend, to arrange a parachute drop. My father called me into his study. He said, 'There is something wrong here. You lead a very strange life. You tell us that you are working at the university until midnight every night. It's not true,*

I can't believe that. Just tell me, is it personal or political? That is all I want to know.' I told him 'Political.' He simply said, 'Good'... And he said, 'Go get packed and I'll send you your mother'...

I lived underground. I stayed everywhere - in hotels, with friends. We extended our network through contacts; people led me to people they knew were trustworthy who wanted to fight the Nazis... [Brigitte learned to use a gun and to fight in unarmed combat.]

One of our key jobs was to select locations for the drops and landings. To do that we used Michelin maps. We looked for areas in the countryside, farmers' meadows, land that was far from the road, far from the electrical lines. (A lot of farmers let us use their meadows and agreed to hide caches of arms.) I would take the co-ordinates of the proposed dropping zones (DZ) and landing zones (LZ) and the number of the Michelin map, and I would code this information, cipher the co-ordinates and send this by radio transmitter to London... ❞ **(B)**

(Quoted in Shelley Saywell, *Women in War*, D.J. Costello, 1985)

Jeanne Bohec was parachuted into France. She had been trained in England to use explosives. When she landed in Brittany the Maquis leaders were amazed - they had not been told she was a women!:

❝ *I taught my first student, a young man, everything he needed to know about making explosives in about two hours. In the following weeks I instructed about ten other men. I even taught a priest sabotage techniques. He was later caught and horribly tortured. The Gestapo tore out his eyes and then shot him.* **(C)**

(Quoted in Shelley Saywell, *Women in War*, D.J. Costello, 1985)

Brigitte and Jeanne met. Brigitte tells us what it was like to live in constant fear:

We were frightened a lot. When we were sitting in a restaurant, if someone just casually looked at us, we thought it was the Gestapo. **(D)**

(Quoted in Shelley Saywell, *Women in War*, D.J. Costello, 1985)

In 1944 it seemed that the war was coming to its end. The Maquis in the South of France mounted raids against the Germans. In revenge the Gestapo and German storm-troopers, the SA, waged a campaign of terror. The Germans rounded up thousands of suspects who were tortured, jailed, sent to concentration camps or shot. Brigitte's luck finally ran out, and she was

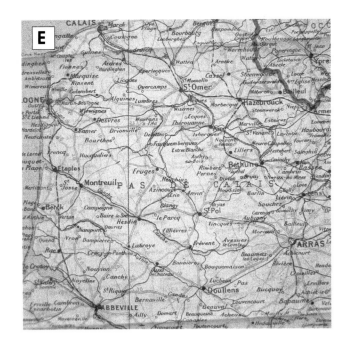

captured in Paris after a chase in which she was shot. Despite heavy torture she refused to talk, and was sent to Ravensbruck, a concentration camp. Most of her friends died, but she lived to tell her tale.

Resistance!

What might it be like to belong to the Resistance? You can create a story about it using sources **A-E**. You can split the scenes up among you, and make a group or class presentation.

1 Building the picture (AT3)

a If you were to interview Brigitte and Jeanne for a school magazine, what might they tell you about their life in the Resistance?

b Your story will cover these points, taken from **B-D**. The parachute drop will take place in **E**.
• people - French, Germans, Gestapo and SA, British
• joining the Resistance
• Mum and Dad find out
• learning codes
• learning to fight
• planning a parachute drop - choosing somewhere in **E** to drop supplies (use the advice in **B** to choose a site)
• sending a radio message about a drop - work out a code and a message to send
• waiting for news of a drop
• waiting for a parachute drop
• a sabotage mission - planning it and carrying it out
• being stopped and searched
• arrest
• torture, jail, journey to a concentration camp

c If working as a group, choose two or more of these scenes, find out what you can about them from your sources and other reading and build up a picture of what might have gone on.

2 Presenting the story (AT2, AT1)

a The story can take a written or spoken form. It should cover the scenes above and include the following:
• Introduction - set the scene about the Maquis.
• the story - work out a plot, split it into sections, describe characters involved.
• Conclusion - link the story into the history of the Resistance.

b Work out the order in which the scenes will occur, and take turns to tell your parts of the story.

ACTIVITY · ACTIVITY

The Battle of Britain

A

What idea of Dowding do you think the artist wants you to have?

What do these names mean to you: Drake, Nelson, Wellington and Dowding? Which battle or campaign does each remind you of, and why did it matter? I doubt if any of you have heard of Dowding (**A**), yet I think he played the main part in winning the Battle of Britain in 1941. Dowding directed and planned the air battle which stopped the German air force, the Luftwaffe, from defeating the RAF (Royal Air Force). What was the Battle of Britain about? After beating France, England was Hitler's only remaining enemy. In the summer of 1941 Hitler drew up plans to invade Britain, Operation Sealion. For Operation Sealion to take place Germany had to control the skies because the German navy was too small and too weak to beat the British navy. With control over the skies, the German air force would sink the British navy and German landing craft could then cross the channel without British ships sinking or bombing them.

Dowding commanded the Royal Air Force in 1941 in the Battle of Britain, the life and death struggle against the Luftwaffe (see the *Factfile*).

B

The Battle of Britain was between British fighter aircraft and German bombers and fighters. England had the Hurricane and Spitfire fighters, the Germans the Messerschmitt 108 (**B**) and 109. The battle was fought out over the skies of southern England (**C**).

Magazine Idol

Pop magazines often contain an account of an 'idol' or a popstar. You can make Sir Hugh Dowding into your idol.

1 Finding out, noting (AT3, AT1)
a Find out what you can about the Battle of Britain and Sir Hugh Dowding.
b Use your sources to note down the things you would like to include in your account of your idol.

2 Writing the account (AT2, AT1)
Your account of your idol should include:
• Dowding's picture, with a caption and one sentence which gets your main idea about him across
• a short account of his part in the Battle
• an outline of the Battle, what was involved in fighting it and why Britain won
• why winning the Battle of Britain was vital

3 Points of view (AT2)
What criticism do you think a Luftwaffe pilot or a fan of Churchill might make of your account of your idol?

ACTIVITY · ACTIVITY

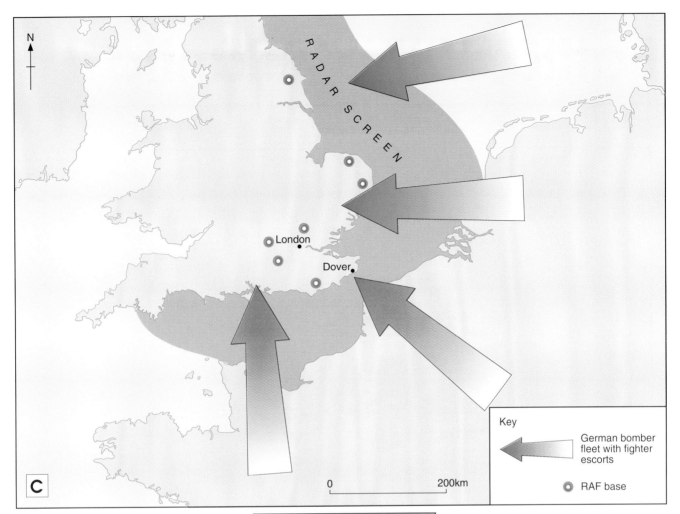

June 1940 Dowding refused to send RAF fighters to France against Churchill's wishes. Fighters kept back to fight against a German invasion. France surrenders.

2 July 1940 German High Command gives orders to get ready to invade Britain. Channel to be made safe for German shipping. Luftwaffe ordered to destroy the RAF. Dowding decides to fight a **defensive** campaign from the safety of his air bases in England. Dowding had the big advantage of radar to pinpoint German attacks.

10 July Luftwaffe bombs shipping in the Channel. Start of the Battle of Britain. Britain has 656 fighters in service.

12 August Luftwaffe switches to bombing British fighter bases in the South and South-East. Destroys many British aircraft but loses far more German bombers.

15 August Luftwaffe loses 76 aircraft, RAF far fewer.

1-5 September Luftwaffe switches attack to inland fighter bases and aircraft factories. Loses sight of destroying the RAF.

7 September Luftwaffe begins heavy daylight bombing of London. Huge bomber raids with fighter escorts lead to heavy German losses.

15 September Luftwaffe's heaviest daylight raid – loses 56 aircraft.

5 October End of daylight bombing.

End October Battle of Britain is over. Britain has 665 fighters in service. Great British victory.

25 November Churchill sacks Dowding.

Aircraft losses	British	German	
		Germans admit	British claim
July	58	164	203
August	360	662	1133
September	361	582	1108
October	136	325	254
TOTAL	915	1733	2698

Battle of the Atlantic

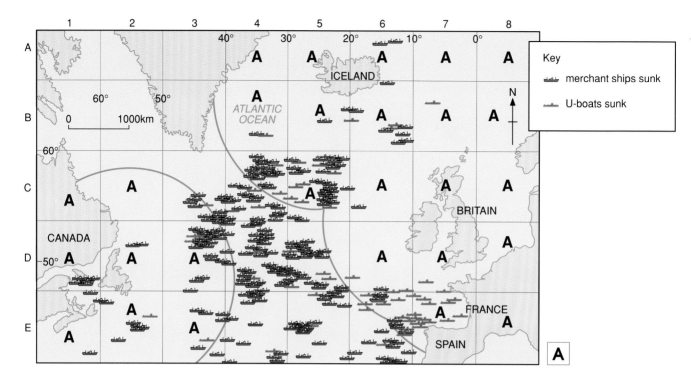

Do you think you will ever starve to death? Between 1941 and 1944 your grandparents could have died of hunger. Why? By midsummer Germany had overrun Belgium, Denmark, France, Holland, Luxemburg and Norway. This meant that Germany's submarines could now strike from French ports like Brest at British shipping coming across the Atlantic.

Throughout 1942 and 1943 Britain, with America's help, used warships and planes to sink more and more submarines. By 1944 Britain was winning the Battle of the Atlantic. How?

- Our ships and planes could find enemy submarines using huff-duff, a new machine to find U-boats, and small radar sets.
- Once found, an underwater bomb or depth charge might sink the submarine.
- Nearly all British ships sailed in convoys, that is kept together. This made it harder for the Germans to sink them.
- The Allies bombed the German submarine bases.
- Hitler built far too few submarines to win the Battle of the Atlantic. He did not think submarine warfare mattered.
- More and more Allied ships were built to replace those the Germans sunk (B).

FACTFILE

- Hitler had cut British shipping off from the whole of Europe.
- German submarines could sink the merchant ships that brought food to Britain (A).
- German submarines used French ports to raid into the Atlantic and long distance planes to spot British ships.
- In 1941 and 1942 the Germans sank more British ships than could be built.
- Food was short in Britain, and had to be rationed.

British merchant ships sunk by U-boats 1941-3

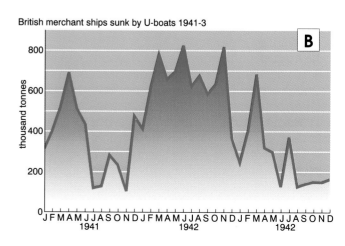

C

Atlantic!

We can use the game battleships to see what impact sailing in convoys had upon the Battle of the Atlantic. The game is for two or three players. If two, one player represents the Germans the other the British. If three, two players represent one side, one the other.

1 To play for 1941 (AT1)
a The British have ten ships leaving New York. Ships can move **two** squares each round in **any** direction. Using map **A**, note down which squares the ships are in (no more than **two** ships in any one square).
b The Germans have ten submarines. They can place **one** or **two** submarines in any one square. Note down which squares they are in. At the end of the round, the sinking chart shows what happens:

No of submarines in square	British ships in square	Submarines sunk	British ships sunk
1	1	0	1
1	2	0	1
2	1 or 2	0	All

c Play the game for five rounds.
d See how many British ships are left.

2 To play for 1943 (AT1)
By 1943 British ships were sailing in groups or convoys, as in **C**, with destroyer and plane escorts. Why do you think it was better for ships to sail in a convoy than singly?
a The British have two convoys of ten ships in each leaving New York with destroyers as escorts.

A convoy can move **two** squares each round in any direction. Note down which squares the convoys are in, no more than **one** convoy in any one square.
b The Germans have ten submarines. They can place a wolf pack of up to ten submarines in any square. Allied air cover now reaches over the squares marked **A**. No German submarines can enter these squares. At the end of the round, if the convoy is in the same square as a German submarine or submarines the following happens:

Number of submarines	Submarines sunk	British ships sunk
1	1	0
2	1	0
3	1	0
4	1	0
5	1	0
6	2	1
7	2	1
8	3	1
9	3	1
10	3	2

c Play the game for five rounds.
d See how many British ships are left.
e Compare the results of the two games.

3 Introduction to game (AT1, AT2)
Write an introduction to the game with
• a short history of the Battle of the Atlantic, saying what it was, why it mattered, what its results were
• what the game tells the player about the Battle of the Atlantic

Barbarossa

By June 1941 Hitler controlled most of Europe. What would he do next? Stalin, Russia's leader, did not believe that Hitler would attack him. On 25 June Moscow journalists sent newsflashes like 1 to their newspapers in Britain and Germany.

NEWSFLASH 1 *25 June 1941*

Germany has attacked Russia to wipe out communism and to gain land on which to settle Germans. German tanks and planes are reported to be invading on a broad front. There is no news about how well the Russians are doing, although the Germans claim that they are meeting little resistance and that the Russians are even welcoming their advance. The Russian air force seems to have been destroyed on the ground.

NEWSFLASH 2 *2 October 1941*

German armies roll forward on three fronts, in the North towards Leningrad, in the centre towards Moscow and in the South towards Rostov. They have captured the Dnieper basin, Russia's richest farming region and its main area for mining and heavy industry. In the North the city of Leningrad, Russia's second largest and its northern capital, is surrounded. Some two million Russians are German prisoners. The Russians have lost around 3000 tanks and 10,000 heavy guns. But, the Russians have managed to take apart and move most of their factories to the East, some 1500 in all.

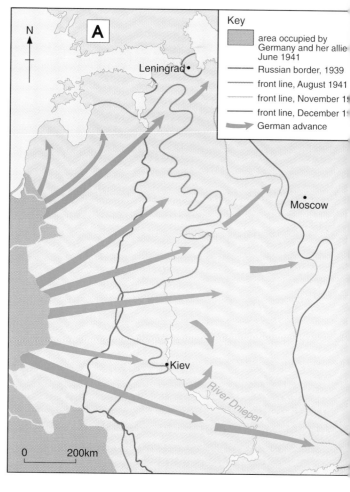

Key

- area occupied by Germany and her allies June 1941
- Russian border, 1939
- front line, August 1941
- front line, November 1941
- front line, December 1941
- German advance

NEWSFLASH 3 *25 December 1941*

The German attacks have ground to a halt. German troops are bogged down and freezing to death outside Moscow and Leningrad. They have no proper winter clothing and equipment to fight in snow and ice. Zhukov, the Russian commander, is attacking the Germans outside Moscow and forcing them back.

Front Page!

Newsflashes can give you an idea of how things change in war. You can prepare the front page for either a British or a German newspaper for one, two or three of the newsflashes. Work on your own or in pairs/threes.

1 Researching and planning (AT1, AT3)
a Use **A** and what else you can find out about Barbarossa, the name for the German attack on Russia. Think of the questions you would like your front page to answer about the German attack and how the struggle is going.
b List the points that you will make on your front page.

2 The front page (AT2, AT1)
Your front page can have on it: the headline, the main news story, comments on the Russo-German war, a cartoon, a picture with a caption, an interview, a map, an account of the reasons why each side was either winning or losing.

3 Display and discussion (AT1, AT2)
Each pair or group can display its front page(s). One person explains to other class members why their front page is made up in the way it is, the other circulates the room looking at other front pages.

The Siege of Leningrad

In a case on the wall of the museum were the faded pages of Tanya's notebook. Tanya was your age.

Zhenya died on 28th December, 12.30 in the morning, 1941

Babushka died on 25th January, 3 o'clock, 1942

Leka died on 17th March, 5 o'clock in the morning, 1942

Dedya Vaya died on 13th April, 2 o'clock at night, 1942

Dedya Lesh on 10th May, 4 o'clock in the afternoon, 1942

Mama on 13th May, 7.30 a.m. 1942

Savchers died. All died. Only Tanya remains. **(A)**

We all felt like crying. Can you think why? How would you feel if your family was wiped out, like Tanya's, in the course of a year? You are only reading this because Tanya's family and a million other inhabitants of Leningrad died in its three-year siege which began in 1941. The Siege of Leningrad was part of the Russian struggle against Hitler which led to Germany's defeat.

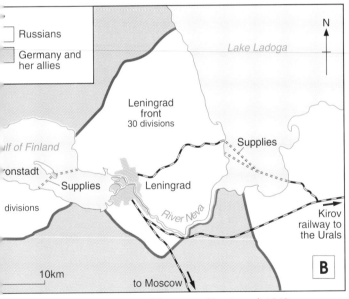

The siege of Leningrad, 1942

By November 1941 Hitler's army had surrounded Leningrad. Food could only reach the city across the frozen lake Ladoga in the winter or by air (map **B**). The ice road was dangerous - bombs and shells wrecked lorries and many fell through the ice. The Germans shelled Leningrad for the next three years. Food was rationed. **C** shows what you would have to eat each day, about a quarter of what you would need:

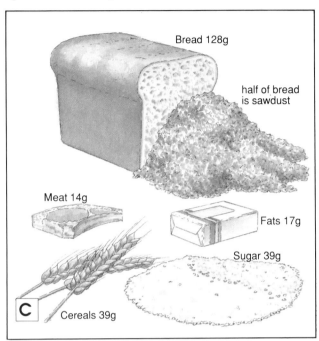

The siege ended in 1944.

Museum

You have to prepare a museum display on the Siege of Leningrad, with Tanya's diary as the main exhibit.

1 Questions and points, finding out (AT1, AT3)
Draw up a list of questions you will answer from the text, sources **A-C** and anything else you can find out about the siege.

2 The exhibition (AT2, AT1)
a Write a short introduction to your exhibition about the Siege of Leningrad. Mention: when, where, what it was, why it mattered.
b Select your sources, and provide a title and a caption for each one.
c Mount your display on a single sheet of paper.
d Put up a class display of your exhibits.

The Russian Campaign

This page shows the horrors of war. The Germans gave orders that food should be sent to Germany even if this meant Russians starved to death. Worse, the Germans thought that the Russians, like the Jews (see pages 62-65) were no better than farm animals. The Germans forced some 3,000,000 Russians to work as slave labour.

I am not interested in the slightest that 10,000 Russian females die of exhaustion digging an anti-tank ditch for us, provided the ditch is dug. **(A)**

(Himmler, a German leader, speaking in 1941)

The Germans destroyed over 70,000 Russian villages and hundreds of towns and cities. Behind German lines bands of partisans fought a fierce and bloody guerilla campaign. The Germans killed those they caught (**B**).

Some 20-25 million Russians died in the war. **C** gave me an idea of what the Germans did:

[Nadya Popova was a Russian pilot flying from a landing strip near the front line. Nadya tells of meeting an old woman in the spring of 1944.] The woman's clothes were in rags. She carried a small basket of berries which she had picked in the forest to feed herself. It was clear that she was starving... She said, 'Please take revenge for me on the Germans. They killed my husband, burned my village to the ground. I have no home, no family, nothing is left. I have been living with the partisans in the forest. I don't know what has happened to my three sons, who left to join the army.' Some children came up to her and stared at us. They were also living with the partisans because they were orphans. **(C)**

Germans hanging Russian partisans.

War Crime!

After the Second World War many Germans were tried for war crimes. You can make out a chart of war crimes, with the evidence you would produce, using this page.

Filling in the chart (AT1, AT3)
Use the facts and your imagination to make out the following chart of accusations against the German numbered 1 in **B**. Put down what crimes he might have carried out, the evidence for them, what witnesses like Nadya Popova and the woman in C might tell you, and the German's defence. Mention:

• what the Germans did to partisans

• what the Germans did to Jews (see pages 64-65)

• how the Germans treated towns

• what the Germans did to villages

• German treatment of the woman and her family in C.

Russian Victory

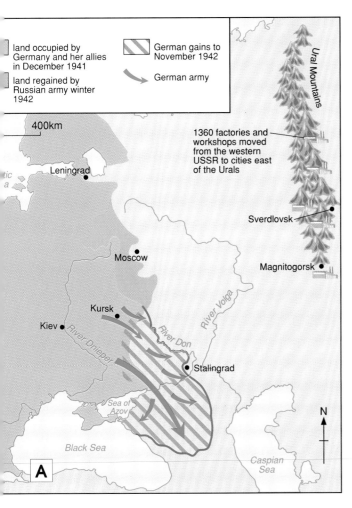

Legend:
- land occupied by Germany and her allies in December 1941
- land regained by Russian army winter 1942
- German gains to November 1942
- German army

400km

1360 factories and workshops moved from the western USSR to cities east of the Urals

Ural Mountains

Leningrad

Sverdlovsk

Moscow

Magnitogorsk

Kursk

Kiev

River Volga

River Don

River Dnieper

Stalingrad

Sea of Azov

Black Sea

Caspian Sea

N

A

Once the German advance ground to a halt in the winter of 1941 fresh Russian armies began to force the Germans back, although in the summer of 1942 the Germans advanced to Stalingrad (**A**). Why did the Russians win?

- The Russians had new, young generals who worked out how to beat the Germans.
- Russia now had more troops and modern tanks, lorries, heavy guns and aircraft than the Germans. The Russian T34 tank outgunned the German Panzers.
- Russia's factories in Siberia poured out a flood of weapons. The factories were out of the range of German bombers.
- In late 1942 a huge German army was cut off at Stalingrad and it surrendered in February 1943. Its men were starving to death and dressed in rags.

- At Kursk in July and August 1943 the Russians smashed the main German army in a huge tank battle.

Kursk meant Hitler had lost the war. The Russian army pushed on towards Berlin. I found useful A.J.P. Taylor's account of how the Russian army fought.

> *At the head came the elite forces: tanks, artillery, rockets, men of high professional competence and technique. Once a breakthrough had been achieved the inexhaustible mass of infantry followed like a barbarian horde on the march: ill-trained, often undisciplined, and living off the country. Crusts of bread and raw vegetables were their only food. They could advance for as much as three weeks without receiving supplies... These Russians slaughtered the German infantry, pillaged the towns and villages through which they passed and raped the women.* **(B)**

(A.J.P. Taylor, *The Second World War*, Hamish Hamilton/Rainbird, 1975)

Victory Monument

Outside Moscow is a monument to the victory over Germany. You can design a wall display to celebrate the Russian defeat of Germany from 1942-45.

1 Finding out (AT3)
Find out what you can about the Russian victory and, using the text and sources, decide what points you will include in your display.

2 Designing the monument (AT2, AT1)
a Draw up a plan for your display.
b List in detail the things that you will want the artist to include in the display.
c Explain the point of view that you want the display to get across.
d As a class you can hold a contest to see which display design you think is the best, and why.

ACTIVITY · ACTIVITY

The Desert Campaign

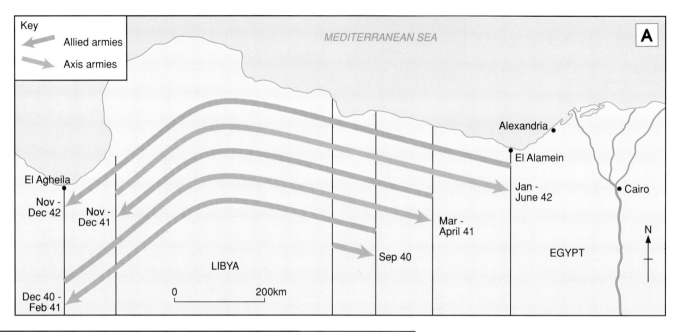

Key
Allied armies
Axis armies

MEDITERRANEAN SEA

A

Alexandria

El Alamein

El Agheila

Nov - Dec 42

Nov - Dec 41

Jan - June 42

Cairo

Mar - April 41

Dec 40 - Feb 41

LIBYA

Sep 40

EGYPT

N

0   200km

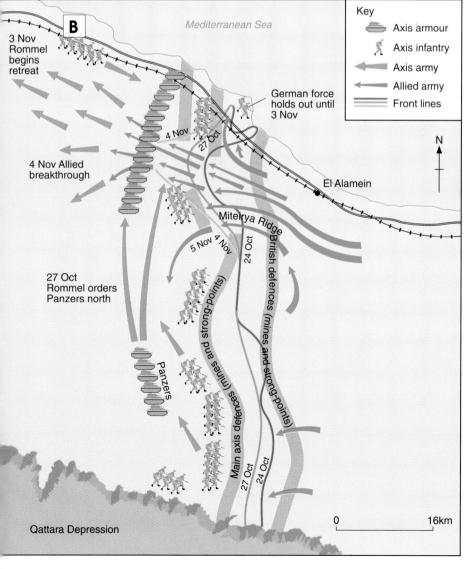

B

Mediterranean Sea

Key
Axis armour
Axis infantry
Axis army
Allied army
Front lines

3 Nov Rommel begins retreat

German force holds out until 3 Nov

4 Nov

27 Oct

4 Nov Allied breakthrough

N

El Alamein

Miteirya Ridge

5 Nov 4 Nov 24 Oct

British defences (mines and strong-points)

27 Oct Rommel orders Panzers north

Main axis defences (mines and strong-points)

Panzers

27 Oct 24 Oct

0   16km

Qattara Depression

In 1941-42, while Tanya's family in Leningrad starved to death and Russia was fighting for its life, a fierce war raged in North Africa between the British and the Axis soldiers of Italy and Germany. The Axis army aimed to capture Egypt, the Suez Canal and then the Middle East oilfields. Can you think why? First the Axis and then the British would push the other side back hundreds of kilometres (see **A**). What problems might the British and Axis forces have with kilometres of stony and sandy desert between them and their bases? By the summer of 1942 the Axis troops needed one more push to reach the Nile. If they could break through at El Alamein the British were finished.

In August 1942 the new British commander, Montgomery, knew that the next battle at El Alamein could decide who would win the war in the Middle East. Map **B** shows the problems he faced. Montgomery laid out his ideas clearly:

> *First - to punch a hole in the enemy position. Second - to pass 10 Corps, strong in armour and mobile troops through this hole into enemy territory. Third - then to develop operations so as to destroy Rommel's [the German commander] forces.* **(C)**

(The Memoirs of Field-Marshal Montgomery, Collins, 1958)

How good a general would you make? For each problem listed below, what advice would you have given Montgomery?

1 When to fight? The British Prime Minister, Winston Churchill, demanded an attack on the Germans and Italians as soon as possible. A victory would be a great boost to the fed up British public. Montgomery did not think the British army was ready to attack at El Alamein. It did not have enough tanks and guns and the troops were not fit or trained to fight a hard battle. This would take at least a month, perhaps two. Should he attack in:

1a August **1b** September **1c** October
1d November?

2 Where to punch the hole (see **B** and **C**)? The front line spread out over 70 kilometres. In the middle was the Miteirya ridge. On the right was the sea, on the left an area of soft sand which tanks could not pass through - the Qattara depression. In the past the British or Axis tank attacks had been either on the left or right. After breaking through the enemy lines the forces wheeled in behind the enemy. Should the British attack on:

2a the left **2b** the right **2c** the centre

3 Who to attack? Montgomery could make his main attack on the Italians *or* Germans *or* both, *or* he could try and prise them apart and then attack one or the other. Should he:

3a attack both **3b** attack the Italians **3c** attack the Germans **3d** prise them apart

4 How to deceive the enemy? Should he go to enormous trouble to build dummy supply dumps, tanks and lorries to trick the Axis into thinking he was going to attack in another place *or* should he try and keep the preparations as secret as possible?

4a trick the Axis **4b** keep the attack secret

Montgomery was ready by the eve of El Alamein. He had 290,000 troops facing 80,000 Axis men and 1200 British tanks against 540 German and Italian. The Germans were short of petrol, Montgomery was well supplied. How do you think the battle went?

El Alamein was a great British victory and the British swept on towards Tunis. With the Americans also landing in North Africa on 8 November 1942 and the British advancing from Egypt, during 1943 the British and Americans (the Allies) drove the Axis forces from Africa.

In 1943 the Allies began to fight their way up Italy. They also got ready to invade Europe from Britain.

Alamein!

How well do you think you would have done as Montgomery's adviser? Work on your own, in pairs or threes.

Thinking through the battle, your battle plan (AT2, AT1)

a Draw up your own plan for the battle, using these headings with your reasons: When To Fight; Where to Punch the Hole; Who to Attack; How to Deceive the Enemy.
b Compare it with the list below, which shows what Montgomery did.
c Write a speech which you would deliver to your troops before the battle began. Mention:
• why the Axis forces had to be beaten
• why you would win
• what the victory would mean to the people of Britain
• your hopes for the rest of the campaign
d Work out how you would give your talk. Think of gestures, how you would stand, the voice you would use.
e Then, as a class, have a contest to see who gives the best speech (the maximum amount of time is two minutes per person).

1c, 2c, 3d, 4a

D-Day

I took sources **A-C** and the *Factfile* from my D-Day scrapbook. In June 1944 on D(elivery)-Day the Allies invaded Europe. The invasion plan was called Operation Overlord.

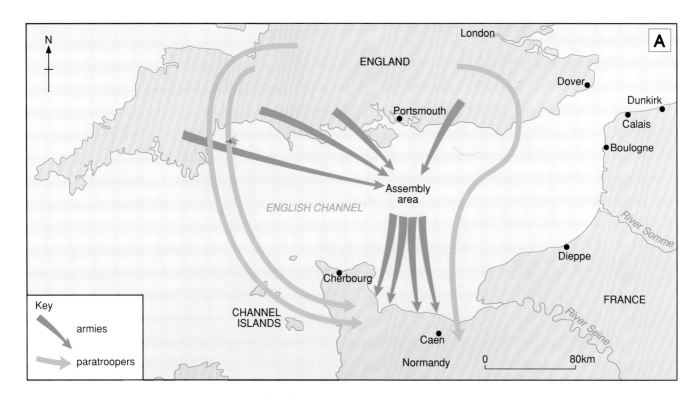

A

Key
armies
paratroopers

London
ENGLAND
Dover
Dunkirk
Calais
Portsmouth
Boulogne
ENGLISH CHANNEL
Assembly area
River Somme
Dieppe
Cherbourg
FRANCE
CHANNEL ISLANDS
River Seine
Caen
Normandy
0   80km

FACTFILE

Operation Overlord

• **Background** In the summer of 1944 Hitler knew that the Allies would invade north-west Europe from England (see map **A**).

• Hitler had a 5000 kilometre coastline to guard, and he felt that the best chance of victory would be to defeat the Allies on the beaches.

• The Germans fortified the beaches with mines, barbed wire, obstacles, gun sites and tank traps. Inland, German teams of tanks were poised ready to push the Allies back into the sea.

• The German agents in Britain sent back messages to Hitler which gave the idea that the Allied attack would come near Calais.

• All the agents were under British control and this plan to deceive the Germans worked. The Allies trained a huge army in the south of England.

• By June the army was ready to land on five beaches in Normandy.

• The Allies would bring with them a Mulberry (floating) harbour and PLUTO, the Pipeline Under the Ocean.

• A German force of Panzer tanks was near Caen (map **B**).

• The Allied plan was that the British were to fight

the Panzers to a standstill.

• The Americans from Utah and Omaha beaches would then swing around behind them and trap them.

• The Allies were then to push on towards Paris and the Seine.

• The Germans did not expect an attack in early June - the weather was foul.

• **6 June** The weather got slightly better. The Allied fleet of around 5000 ships set sail.

• After heavy bombing and shelling of the Normandy beaches, the Allies landed the first of 150,000 men and 1500 tanks. Paratroops seized key points.

• Hitler still thought that the main attack would come near Calais.

9 July It took a month to beat the German forces at Caen and push towards the Seine.

• **August** The Allies failed to trap the main German army in the Falaise pocket which escaped and streamed back towards Germany.

• **September** Most of France was in Allied hands. The attack on Germany from the West was about to begin.

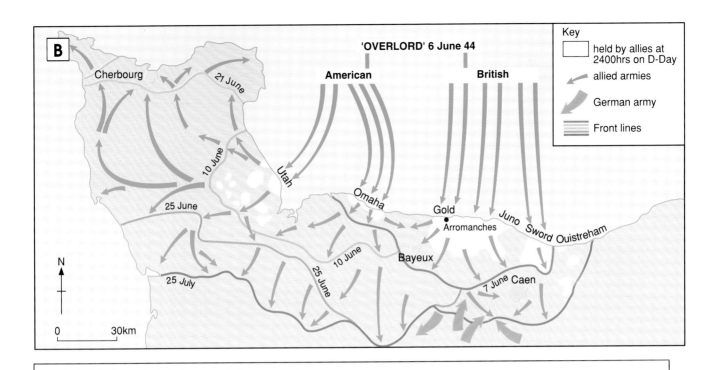

B

'OVERLORD' 6 June 44

American   British

Key

held by allies at 2400hrs on D-Day

allied armies

German army

Front lines

Cherbourg

21 June

10 June

25 June

Utah

Omaha

Gold
Arromanches

Juno Sword Ouistreham

Bayeux

25 July

25 June

10 June

7 June Caen

N

0   30km

D-Day Diary

You can use sources **A-C** and the *Factfile* to create a D-Day diary on your own, as a group or as a class.

1 Research (AT3)

a Find out what you can about D-Day.

b Interview any old people about what they know. They might even have a diary or newspaper and magazine you might borrow.

c Look at as many books, pictures and magazines as you can find.

d Pick out your favourite pictures, drawings or story about D-Day to put in your diary.

2 Studying the sources (AT3, AT1)

a Study **C**. For points **1-6** say one thing that is a fact, and one question you would like to ask about that point. Pool your facts and questions.

b If you were able to interview one of the soldiers at **one** of points 1-6, what might he tell you about the last 24 hours.

c Brainstorm what might happen to any of the soldiers in the next hour, six hours, twelve hours.

d Study **A** and **B**. If you were one of the soldiers **1-6** on **C**, what might have happened to you on these days: 4, 5, 6, 7 June, 7 July, 16, 19 August?

3 D-Day diary (AT1, AT2)

Prepare your own D-Day diary from the point of view of either a British or American soldier who took part in the D-Day landing.

a Decide which person you would like to be.

b You can split the days in **2d** up among you, and write your diary entry for one or more of these days.

c Base what you write on what you have learned about D-Day. You can include pictures, maps and drawings.

d Write out your diary entry or entries, each with its date and place.

e Put them up or read them out in date order.

f What view do they give of D-Day? How true are they likely to be?

ACTIVITY · ACTIVITY

C

5 2 3 6 4 1

Victory in Europe

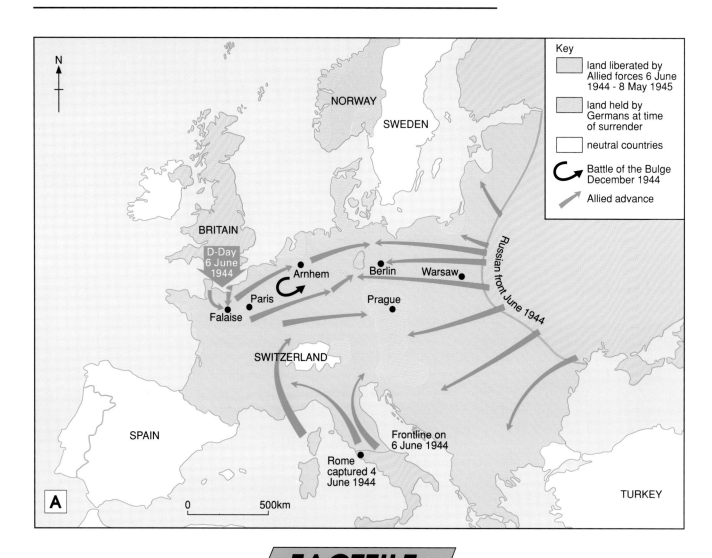

Key
- land liberated by Allied forces 6 June 1944 - 8 May 1945
- land held by Germans at time of surrender
- neutral countries
- ↺ Battle of the Bulge December 1944
- ↗ Allied advance

NORWAY

SWEDEN

BRITAIN

D-Day 6 June 1944

Arnhem

Berlin

Warsaw

Paris

Prague

Falaise

Russian front June 1944

SWITZERLAND

SPAIN

Frontline on 6 June 1944

Rome captured 4 June 1944

TURKEY

A

0   500km

N

FACTFILE

June/July 1944	Operation Overlord - Allied landing in the West in Normandy. In Eastern Europe Russians smash the main German army and take 350,000 prisoners.
August	Allied forces land in the South of France - Operation Anvil. Paris liberated. Russians reach Warsaw.
September	Finland and Romania make peace with Russia.
October	Bulgaria surrenders to the Russians.
December	German counter-attack in the West at the Ardennes fails. This attack is called the Battle of the Bulge as it occurred at a bulge in the Allied frontline.
January 1945	Allies drive on into Germany. Russians take Warsaw. Main

Russian attack on Germany starts.

February	British continue heavy bombing of German cities, hoping this will stop the German people from wanting to fight. One of the 1000 bomber raids burns German city of Dresden full of refugees to a cinder in a firestorm **(C)**. Berlin and other cities are also in ruins. Germans are starving to death.
March	British and Americans cross the Rhine. Russians approach Berlin.
April	Russian and Allied troops meet at Torgau.
30 April	Hitler marries Eva Braun, his mistress, and then shoots himself. The two events were not linked.
May	Germany and Italy surrender.

Map **A** gives you some idea of how the rest of the war went. It is easy to think of Germany's defeat as a great British and American victory, with the Russians also rolling up German armies in Eastern Europe as a bit of an afterthought. The truth is that it was the Russians who beat the mighty German armies in 1942 and 1943. In 1944-45 the Russians still faced the main German fighting force. The *Factfile* lists the main events of 1944/45.

Montgomery, the British commander, tells the story of the German surrender in the West:

> *They [the German generals] were brought to my caravan site and were drawn up under the Union Jack, which was flying proudly in the breeze. I kept them waiting for a few minutes and then came out of my caravan and walked towards them* **(D)**. *They all saluted, under the Union Jack. It was a great moment; I knew the Germans had come to surrender and that the war was over... I said to my interpreter, 'Who are these men?' He told me. I then said, 'What do they want?'* [*The Germans also offered to surrender the German armies who were fighting the Russians to the British.*] *Von Friedeburg said it was unthinkable to surrender to the Russians as they were savages, and the German soldiers would be sent straight off to work in Russia. I said the Germans should have thought of all these things before they began the war, and particularly before they attacked the Russians in June 1941.* **(B)**

(3 May 1945, *The Memoirs of Field Marshal Montgomery*)

With Germany's surrender the war effort now switched to the Far East, where America, Britain and Russia faced Japan, see pages 56-57.

Victory Broadcast!

News of victory brought relief to the German and great joy to the British, American and Russian peoples. On 5 May 1945 what kind of radio news programme might have been broadcast from Montgomery's camp to America, Britain, Germany and Russia when the Germans surrendered? You can take the role of either an American, British, German or Russian broadcaster. Work on your own, in pairs, threes or larger groups.

1 Researching and planning (AT3, AT1)
a Using **A** and **C** and what you can find out, work out how the campaign against Germany went from June 1944-May 1945.
b Describe the part played by American, British and Russian forces and the bombing of German cities **(C)**.
c Give reasons for the Germans' defeat.
d Use **B** and **D** to describe the meeting, and what went on afterwards. You can take roles and act out the scene.
e List and discuss the problems which you think Europe had in May 1945.

2 The broadcast (AT2, AT1)
Prepare, rehearse and tape or read out your broadcast. It can include interviews.

Pearl Harbor

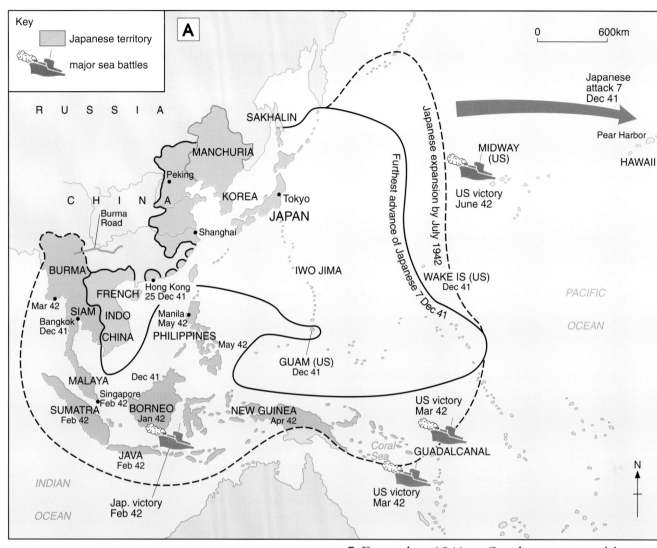

Key
- Japanese territory
- major sea battles

RUSSIA

SAKHALIN

MANCHURIA

• Peking

KOREA

• Tokyo

JAPAN

CHINA

Burma Road

• Shanghai

Furthest advance of Japanese 7 Dec 41

Japanese expansion by July 1942

Japanese attack 7 Dec 41

MIDWAY (US)
US victory June 42

Pear Harbor

HAWAII

IWO JIMA

BURMA

Mar 42

FRENCH

Hong Kong 25 Dec 41

WAKE IS (US) Dec 41

PACIFIC

SIAM

Bangkok Dec 41

INDO

Manila May 42

CHINA

PHILIPPINES

May 42

OCEAN

MALAYA

Dec 41

GUAM (US) Dec 41

Singapore Feb 42

BORNEO Jan 42

NEW GUINEA Apr 42

US victory Mar 42

SUMATRA Feb 42

JAVA Feb 42

Jap. victory Feb 42

Coral Sea

GUADALCANAL

US victory Mar 42

INDIAN

OCEAN

N

0   600km

B

7 December 1941, a Sunday morning like any other at Pearl Harbor, Hawaii, America's main navy base in the Pacific (map **A**). America's battleships rested safely at anchor. The radar had shut down, as the operators had gone to a church parade. The operators had noted some planes coming in to land from American aircraft carriers. There seemed to be no problems. Just before 8.00 a.m. things changed (see **B** and *Factfile 1*). Two hours later photograph **C** was taken in the harbour.

Japan was now at war with America and Britain. Japanese forces swept forward, hopping from island to island (see **A**). Japanese troops captured the British bases at Singapore and Malaya and Burma (see *Factfile 2*). By May 1942 the Japanese were poised to strike at India and Australia.

FACTFILE

FACTFILE 1	FACTFILE 2
1941 Japan conquers most of French Indo-China. **July** America, Britain and the Dutch cut off Japan's oil supplies to stop the Japanese advance. This will ruin Japan's economy. Peace talks between Japanese and British and Americans collapse. Germany promises to back Japan in a war. **November-December** Japan gets ready to drive Americans, British and Dutch out of the Far East. Then Japan will attack Singapore. **7 December 1941 8.00 a.m.** Japanese planes attack Pearl Harbor. 360 planes from six Japanese aircraft carriers sink four American battleships, damage four more and sink ten other ships. America's four big aircraft carriers are away from Pearl Harbor. **10.00 a.m.** The Japanese attack is over.	**8 December 1941** Japanese capture Hong Kong, Britain's main base in China. **10 December** Japanese aircraft sink British battleship *Repulse* and aircraft carrier *The Prince of Wales* based at Singapore. End of British sea power in the Far East. **February 1942** Japanese take great British military base at Singapore, the heart of the British empire. 35,000 Japanese capture 80,000 British troops. **January-May** Japanese overrun Borneo, Burma, Dutch East Indies, Malaya, Philippines, Singapore (see **A**). **May** Battle of Coral Sea sees end of Japanese attempt to invade Australia. **4 June Battle of Midway** The key carrier battle of the war. Japanese fleet with eight carriers attacks American fleet with four carriers. American planes sink four largest Japanese carriers. Major Japanese defeat.

C

Magazine!

Prepare a magazine report for *either* an American *or* a Japanese Sunday Magazine on Pearl Harbor. Work on your own, in pairs, threes or a larger group. Prepare copy for each of the points below. Share out the tasks among you.

1 The magazine (AT2, AT1)
a What headline would you put to tell of the Japanese attack on Pearl Harbor?

b What captions would you have for photographs **B** and **C**?
c Briefing - What background story would you write giving the reasons for Pearl Harbor.
d What eye witness account of the attack would you have from the viewpoint of a Japanese pilot, spy or one of the American fire fighters in the boat in **C**.
e Draw or plan out a cartoon about the Japanese attack.
f Timeline - Draw up a timeline to show how the Japanese war went in 1941-42.
• Put the heading, The Japanese War, December 1941-July 1942.
• Down the left-hand side of a clean page

mark the eight months.
• Put on your timeline the main events of the eight months.
g Mapwork - Copy **A** and make cut outs as an overlay to show the size of the Japanese empire in July 1942 and December 1941.

2 Censor (AT2)
If you had produced your magazine in December 1941, a censor would have had to approve what you printed. Look at your group's magazine entries, and then say what changes *either* the Japanese *or* the American censor might have demanded.

Hiroshima and Nagasaki

What is the worst thing that you can think of happening to you and your class? Jot your thoughts down on paper. Work out a class list, and try and put them into an order of awfulness. Then look at **C** and **D** and read **E** and **F**.

In 1943 and 1944 the Americans slowly pushed back the Japanese, 'hopping' from island to island (map **A**). In a number of sea battles the Americans sank the Japanese navy's force of aircraft carriers and battleships. By March 1945 the Americans had captured the Philippines. After a bloody battle they stormed the island of Iwo Jima. Some 7000 Americans died in fierce fighting. In June the Americans took Okinawa.

America planned to invade Japan. Truman (**B**) knew that hundreds of thousands of soldiers would die - the Japanese fought to the death.

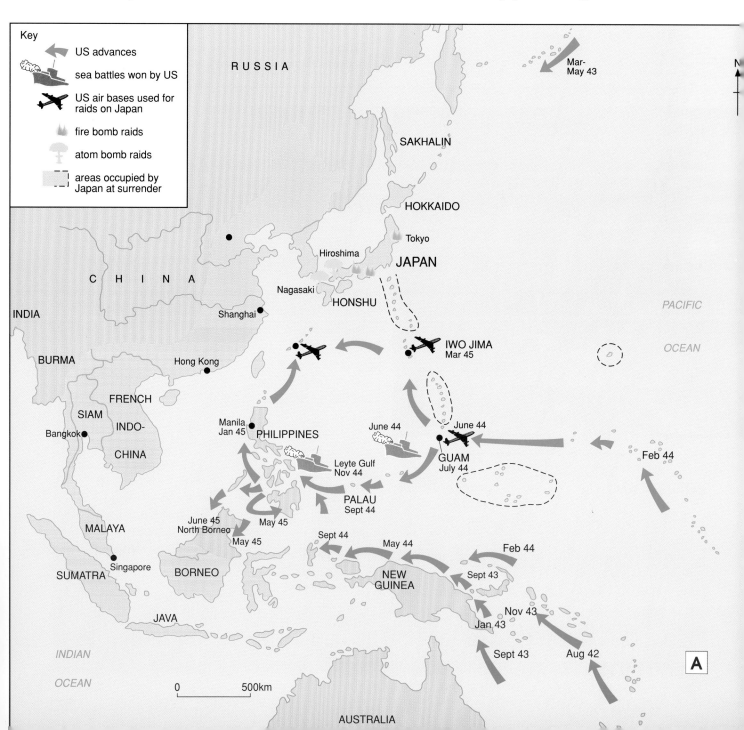

Key

- → US advances
- sea battles won by US
- ✈ US air bases used for raids on Japan
- fire bomb raids
- atom bomb raids
- areas occupied by Japan at surrender

RUSSIA

SAKHALIN

HOKKAIDO

Tokyo

Hiroshima

JAPAN

Nagasaki

HONSHU

CHINA

INDIA

Shanghai

BURMA

Hong Kong

FRENCH

SIAM

INDO-

Bangkok

CHINA

Manila
Jan 45

PHILIPPINES

Leyte Gulf
Nov 44

PALAU
Sept 44

June 45
North Borneo

May 45

May 45

Sept 44

MALAYA

Sept 44

May 44

Feb 44

SUMATRA

Singapore

BORNEO

NEW
GUINEA

Sept 43

JAVA

Nov 43

Jan 43

Sept 43

Aug 42

IWO JIMA
Mar 45

June 44

June 44

GUAM
July 44

Feb 44

PACIFIC

OCEAN

Mar-
May 43

N

INDIAN

OCEAN

0   500km

AUSTRALIA

A

American planes, ships and submarines blockaded Japan. Little food and raw materials now reached her people; they began to starve. By now huge American bomber raids were burning to ashes many Japanese towns and cities like Tokyo. Incendiary bombs would ignite thousands of wooden houses. A huge 'fireball' would follow. The fireball would suck in a gale of air which fanned the flames. Hundreds of thousands of Japanese were burned to death.

Japan fought on, despite Germany's defeat in May.

In July 1945 the American, British and Russian leaders of the Allies met at Potsdam. America had spent a huge amount of money on building the atom bomb, the Manhattan Project. On the day of the Potsdam meeting America tested the atom bomb. A message in code, 'Babies satisfactorily born', reached the American president. The Allies could now drop atom bombs on Japan. They called upon Japan to surrender. If she did not, she was warned of 'prompt and utter destruction'.

The new American president, Harry Truman, tells us what was going through his mind at the time:

A month before the test explosion of the atomic bomb the Joint Chiefs of Staff had laid their detailed plans for the defeat of Japan before me for approval. In all it had been estimated that it would require until the late fall [autumn] of 1946 to bring Japan to her knees. All of us fully realised that the fighting would be fierce and the losses heavy. General Marshal told me that it might cost half a million American lives to force the enemy's surrender on his home ground.

The daily tragedy of a bitter war crowded in on us. We labored to construct a weapon of such overpowering force that the enemy would be forced to yield swiftly once we could resort to it. This was the primary aim of our secret and vast effort. **(B)**

(Harry S. Truman, *Memoirs*)

In August 1945 Truman decided to use his new, powerful weapon, the atom bomb, against Japan. On 6 August an A-bomb was dropped on the city of Hiroshima.

• The bomb went off 300 metres above the ground.

• The blast and heat flattened and burnt all houses in a two-kilometre radius, wrecked those for another two kilometres and broke the windows of all those five to six kilometres away **(C)**.

• The blast, heat, fires and radiation killed about 100,000 people and wounded thousands more. I found sources **E** and **F** about Hiroshima.

• Today people are still dying from the bomb's radiation.

• Six days later a second bomb destroyed Nagasaki **(D)**. About another 75,000 people died.

C

D

Nagasaki after the bomb.

> The hour was early; the morning still, warm and beautiful... Clad in vest and pants, I was sprawled on the living-room floor exhausted because I had just spent a sleepless night on duty as an air-raid warden in my hospital.
>
> Suddenly a strong flash of light startled me - and then another. So well does one recall little things that I remember vividly how a stone lantern in the garden became brilliantly lit and I debated whether this light was caused by a magnesium flare or sparks from a passing train.
>
> Garden shadows disappeared. Where a moment before all had been so bright and sunny it was now dark and hazy. Through swirling dust I could barely discern a wooden column that had supported one corner of my house. It was leaning crazily and the roof sagged dangerously...
>
> I tried to escape, but rubble and fallen timbers barred the way. By picking my way cautiously I managed to reach the roka [passage] and stepped down into my garden. A profound weakness overcame me, so I stopped to regain my strength. To my surprise I discovered that I was completely naked. How odd. Where were my vest and pants?
>
> What had happened?
>
> All over the right side of my body I was cut and bleeding. A large splinter was protruding from a mangled wound in my thigh, and something warm trickled into my mouth. My cheek was torn, I discovered as I felt it gingerly, with the lower lip laid wide open. Embedded in my neck was a sizeable fragment of glass which I matter-of-factly dislodged. 'We'll be all right', [I told my wife] 'Only let's get out of here as fast as we can.' **(E)**

(Michihiko Hichiya, *Hiroshima Diary*, Victor Gollanz, 1955)

> The streets were deserted except for the dead. Some looked as if they had been frozen by death while in the full action of flight; others lay sprawled as though some giant had flung them to their death from a great height. Hiroshima was no longer a city, but a burnt over prairie. **(F)**

(Eye witness visitor, 1945)

Soon after the second bomb was dropped the Japanese emperor decided that Japan must surrender. The war was over.

Atom Bomb Exhibition

You can plan and present an exhibition on the bombing of Hiroshima and Nagasaki. You can each do one of the tasks, 2-6, and then pool your ideas for the exhibition.

1 Researching (AT3)
a Find out what you can about the attack on Hiroshima and Nagasaki and sort out as many pictures, stories and accounts of the bombing as you can find to use in your exhibition.
b Read pages 58-61.
c Work out what message Truman is trying to give you about the bomb in source **B**.
d Think of or list all the things in pictures **C** and **D** that the bomb has done to the cities.
e Look at source **E** and make out a timetable for Michihiko before the bomb went off and straight after.
f What thoughts does **F** give you about the bomb?

2 Background (AT1)
On a copy of **A** mark how the American campaign against Japan was going. Put in:

• the taking of the islands
• cutting off of Japan
• the blockade
• the bombing of the cities - fire-storms
• your plan for invading Japan

3 Reasons for the attack on Hiroshima (AT1, AT2)
If you could interview Harry Truman (**B**) what answer might he give to these questions?
a Why did you drop the bomb?
b Whose advice did you rely on and could you trust it?
c What might have happened if you had not used the bomb?

4 The impact of the bomb (AT1, AT2)
Use pictures **C** and **D** to work out the impact of the bomb.
a Think of your local town or city centre. Work out what might happen within two, four, five to six kilometres if the bomb had been dropped on it.

b Write captions for **C** and **D** to show:

• what the scene might have been before the bomb
• where the bomb might have gone off
• what it did to the buildings (blast, heat, fire)
• the scene one hour, one day and one week after the blast

c What might the person in **C** tell you about the attack.

5 An Hiroshima diary (AT2, AT1)
What kind of diary entry might you write if you had been living in your present home in Hiroshima in August 1945? Mention:

• life before the bomb
• you hear the plane going overhead
• what you would see, hear, feel and smell when the bomb went off and straight afterwards in the house
• what you would see on the street
• what might happen to you during the rest of the day

Include a drawing of yourself showing wounds like those which Michihiko suffered.

6 Arguments about the A-bomb (AT2)
Since 1945 a bitter debate has been going on as to whether it was right to drop the atom bomb on Hiroshima. What answers might there be to these points?

• Japan would have been forced to surrender anyway because of the bombing of her cities and the blockade.
• The killing of innocent citizens is a crime.
• There was no need to bomb Nagasaki.

7 The exhibition (AT1, AT2)
Work out how you would display your materials on a wall or on a large piece of paper or card.

ACTIVITY · ACTIVITY ·

The Holocaust (1)

Slugs are a pest in most gardens, they eat vegetables like cabbages and beans. At night gardeners put down handfuls of slug killer, which does the trick. In the morning there are piles of bodies everywhere. In the same way Hitler and the Nazis behaved towards people whom they thought were not Aryans, members of the German master race. Hitler believed that people like the Slavs of Russia, Gypsies and Jews were subhuman. A Jew who was your age when he lived in Nazi Germany tells us:

> *Anti-Semitism built up from lots of small, separate causes. The Jews are doing well. We're unemployed and they're rich. They killed Jesus (that's a very old one). They're ugly.* **(B)**

(Sir Claus Moser, *The Independent*, 28 July 1992)

One Jewish family was that of Anne Frank. Luckily in 1933 her parents had gone to work in Holland. In the 1930s the Franks thought that they were safe in Holland from the Nazis. They were until May 1940, when Germany conquered Holland. By the autumn of 1941 most Jews in Europe were under Nazi rule. What did Nazi rule mean for the Franks? Anne at this time was about your age.

> *That is when the sufferings of us Jews really began. Anti-Jewish decrees [orders] followed each other in quick succession:*
> * *Jews must wear a yellow star.*
> * *Jews must hand in their bicycles [today it would be bicycles and cars].*
> * *Jews are banned from trams [buses and trains today] and are forbidden to drive.*
> * *Jews are only allowed to do their shopping between three and five o'clock and then only in shops which bear the sign 'Jewish shop'.*
> * *Jews must be indoors by eight o'clock and cannot even sit in their own gardens after that hour.*
> * *Jews are forbidden to visit theatres, cinemas and other places of entertainment.*
> * *Jews may not take part in public sports.*

Der Stürmer was an anti-semitic Nazi newspaper. Which figures in the picture do you think are Jews? Why are they shown in this way? What do the crows signify? How does the artist portray Germans in the picture? Why?

FACTFILE

* The Jews were the Nazis' main victims for Hitler loathed all Jews.
* For hundreds of years throughout Europe Jews have had to put up with attacks upon them - racial discrimination.
* This anti-semitism reached its height in Nazi Germany **(A)**.
* The Nazis took away **all** Jews' rights. For example, Jews lost their citizenship and jobs and could not own property.
* Jews lived in danger of being jailed or beaten up and even killed by Nazi thugs.
* Many Jews fled to safety abroad.
* Millions of Jews lived mainly in towns and cities spread across Europe. Most Jews' homes were in Poland and Russia.
* When the Germans had conquered most of Europe in 1941 they turned on the Jews and decided to kill them all - the Final Solution.

> * *They are banned from swimming baths, tennis courts, hockey fields and other sports grounds.*
> * *Jews may not visit Christians.*
> * *Jews must go to Jewish schools.* **(C)**

(*The diary of Anne Frank*, Pan Books)

By 1942 the Nazis had begun to carry out a plan to round up all Jews and send them to prison camps. In July Anne Frank's father was told to report to the Germans. He knew he would be arrested and sent to a camp. So, the family went into hiding **(D)** in a secret flat in an office. Source **E** shows where they lived until March 1944.

> *8 July 1942. Margot and I began to pack some of our most vital belongings into a school satchel. The first thing I put in was this diary, then hair-curlers, handkerchiefs, school books, a comb, old letters; I put in the craziest things with the idea that we were going into hiding. But I'm not sorry, memories mean more to me than dresses.* **(D)**

(*The diary of Anne Frank*, Pan Books)

Anne and her family were safe until August 1944. Then the Germans found them. The Germans sent the Franks in cattle trucks to the concentration camps (see page 64).

E

The Franks lived in a flat in the top two floors of the office block. They got into the flat through a swinging cupboard.

(see page 64)

Anti-Semitism

Anti-semitism is one kind of discrimination - people being picked on for what they are. What other kinds can you think of which go on today? You can put yourself in Anne's shoes to try and work out what it is like to be discriminated against.

1 Thinking about discrimination (AT1, AT3)
Put the things in **C** into the order which you would find hardest to take.

2 Discrimination today (AT1, AT2)
What might it be like to be treated like a Jew if Nazi laws were passed today? You can make out two timelines of your life, one for a week and the other for a day.
a Split the page into three columns (see below).
b In the second column put how you spend your time now. In the third column put what you could have done if you were a Jew in Europe in 1942.

Timeline - the past week		
Days of week	What you did	What as a Jew you could have done

Timeline - yesterday		
Hour of the day	What you did	What as a Jew you could have done

c Work out what you would take with you if you were told when you went home tonight that you had to go into hiding and could only pack things in a small bag.
d Look at **E**. Write a diary entry like **D**, and as a class read each other's.

ACTIVITY · ACTIVITY ·

The Holocaust (2)

Sitting around a bonfire in Israel brought home to me what the Holocaust meant. All the people were mourning their dead relations whom the Nazis had slaughtered from 1941-45. **A-F** are clues I chose for you to read, look at and think about to learn about the Holocaust.

❝ *On 3rd September 1944 the Jewish prisoners... were sent, packed in cattle-trucks, eastwards to Auschwitz, the notorious extermination centre in German-occupied Poland ... the older members of the party weakened under the terrible conditions of life in Auschwitz. Van Daan was selected for the gas chamber and put to death. As for the two girls, they had been sent to Bergen-Belsen in Germany two months before their mother's death. In February 1945, both the sisters caught typhus. One day Margot, who was lying in the bunk immediately above Anne's, seeking to rise, lost her hold and fell on to the floor. In her weakened state the shock killed her. Her sister's death did to Anne **(B)** what all her previous sufferings had failed to do: it broke her spirit. A few days later, in early March, she died.* ❞ **(A)**

(Introduction to *The diary of Anne Frank*, Pan)

B

❝ *No monument stands over Babii Yar.*
A drop sheer as a crude gravestone.
I am afraid.
Today I am as old in years
as all the Jewish people.
Now I seem to be a Jew.
Here I plod through ancient Egypt.
Here I perish crucified, on the cross,
and to this day I bear the scars of nails.
I seem to be Dreyfus.
The Philistine is both informer and judge.
I am behind bars.
Beset on every side.
Hounded, spat on, slandered.
Squealing, dainty ladies in flounced Brussels lace
stick their parasols into my face. ❞ **(C)**

(from *Babii Yar* by Yevgeny Yevtushenko)

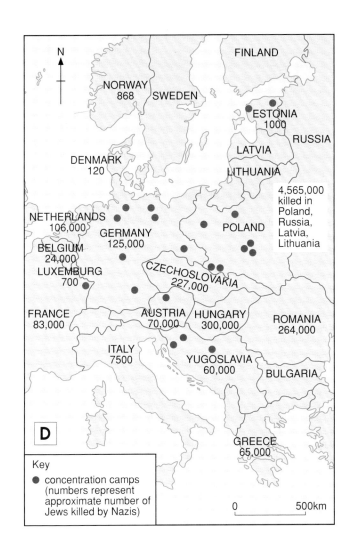

Key
● concentration camps
(numbers represent
approximate number of
Jews killed by Nazis)

0   500km

D

NORWAY 868
SWEDEN
FINLAND
ESTONIA 1000
RUSSIA
LATVIA
LITHUANIA
DENMARK 120
4,565,000 killed in Poland, Russia, Latvia, Lithuania
NETHERLANDS 106,000
GERMANY 125,000
POLAND
BELGIUM 24,000
LUXEMBURG 700
CZECHOSLOVAKIA 227,000
FRANCE 83,000
AUSTRIA 70,000
HUNGARY 300,000
ROMANIA 264,000
ITALY 7500
YUGOSLAVIA 60,000
BULGARIA
GREECE 65,000

E

There are no Activities on this spread. The
evidence speaks for itself.

F

Evacuation

When you get home tonight you find a strange girl in your sitting room. She has come to live with you. How would you feel? In September 1939 millions of families like yours had to put up schoolchildren from the cities.

As war approached fear gripped both the government and people that heavy German bombing would burn Britain's cities. In September began the biggest movement [migration] of people in English history. Children under 11 with their teachers and mothers of the under fives were sent from cities like London to safety in the country.

What was it like to be evacuated?
• The night before you would pack your bags, just like going on holiday.
• Next morning you would take your bags to school (**A**). Don't forget your label with your name on it!
• Buses would take you from school to the station. There you would be loaded on a train to safety (**B**). But where might you be going?
• You would be met at a country or town station, and would walk or be taken by bus, car or cart to your new home.
• Life in the country would be strange, a new home, new school, new people, new things to do.
• The babies and their mums could be happy (**C**). But what about the dads left behind?

Evacuation went smoothly, but the problems came when the evacuees arrived. Most were poor

city kids. How did country children feel? I found **D**, it might give you an idea. In 1975 Raymond Huntingdon lived at Wigton, in Cumbria. He tells us:

> *[One kind of] evacuee came with the short hair-cut. I can remember them. Little wee tags on them, like shifting cattle about. The vast majority were Geordies [from the North-East, Newcastle]... They were alone, to themselves, sort of thing. They were townies as against us country lads... I can't remember any evacuees ever playing in our immediate circle, in, we'll say, eight or ten lads.* **(D)**

(Melvyn Bragg, *Speak For England*, 1977)

When Hector Bolitho came home for a quiet weekend he had an awful shock:

> *The house, once tranquil and orderly, is like a boarding house. Perambulators and cots all over the place and the pungent smell of babies... But the village! The refugees turned out to be unwashed illiterates from Whitechapel. Stanley, the village carter, found six fleas in his clothes after bringing the luggage from the station. The radio told us that the evacuation of the London children had been made without a hitch. Well, it is an unholy mess here. There is bitterness already. The evacuated people moan because there is only one village shop. Some went back on the next bus to London. Marion Craven told me that one of the women stroked her hair and face and said, 'You have kind face. Give bed for me and my child.' Marion gave them a bed, but she said, 'They were so dirty that I went home and had a bath and washed my hair.'* **(E)**

(Hector Bolitho, *War in the Strand*, Secker & Warburg, 1942)

The evacuation meant a huge social mix up. Poor children lived in well-off people's homes, and rich children might end up living in houses without any electricity, running water and with no flush toilet. Within a few months most evacuees went home, the bombing was not as bad as feared. Some stayed, and at the height of the Blitz from September-May 1941 a new wave of refugees came to the country.

Evacuation!

Work on the text and sources and Evacuation! to get some idea of what evacuation meant.

1 Sources (AT3)
Use the sources to think yourself into what it might have been like in 1939.
a What have the girls in **A** got in their bags?
b What might be said at the station (**B**)?
c What thoughts might be going through the mind of the mother in **C**?
d What does **D** suggest about problems you might have living in a strange place?
e In **E** what has happened to Hector's house, and what might Stanley and Marion think about the evacuees?
f What might the woman in **E** and her friends think about their new homes and the village?

2 Evacuation (AT1, AT2)
Write a diary for September 1939 as if you were being evacuated from your home to the country.
Getting ready You have to pack all you need into bags you can carry like those in **A**, and your gasmask. Work out what you would take: a bag of food to last a whole day, your name tag with your name and address. As a class you could bring in what you would take, and see if you have all got the right things!
School and station Saying goodbye to mum and dad. To school. Work out the questions you would ask and talk about with both your friends and teachers. Say what it was like going to the school, what happened there, the buses to the station, the station, the train and its carriage (**B**) leaving.
The journey Think of your last long train journey. Then imagine what it might be like going on such a journey when you are being evacuated. What might you talk about?
Arrival and new home You arrive in the village in **D**. Say what happens to you on your trip from the station to your new home, what you think of the village and its people, your thoughts and fears.

ACTIVITY · ACTIVITY

The Blitz

Think of your worst nightmare. Then compare it with **A**, which contains extracts from the story of an air raid. I picked them to show what a raid like **C** felt like. The *Factfile* gives you some ideas of what the Blitz was about.

66 *17 April 1941. We have been through London's most terrible night. It is not easy to write down anything about it because I still feel as if I have been hit with a mallet... We took the sirens for granted when they sounded about nine o'clock...*

FACTFILE

7 September 1940 German bombing of London begins and lasts for 57 nights in a row.
In 1941 Bombing spreads to other cities and ports in West of England as well as London. Germans also bomb beautiful cities, Baedeker raids, in revenge for English raids on German cities. Germans dropped 2-300 tonnes of bombs per raid. Raids smashed places like City of London **(B)**, East End of London and cities like Coventry. 3,500,000 homes damaged or destroyed.
16 May 1941 Last heavy German raid - on Birmingham. Bombing went on, but the worst of the Blitz was over.

Defence measures
• Use of **barrage balloons**, **searchlights**, **guns** and **fighters** to stop German bombers.
• **Radar** guides guns and fighters.
• Germans used radio beams to guide their bombers. British bent these and bombs fell on open fields.
• To shelter from raids people used **Anderson** and **Morrison shelters** in their homes and gardens, special air-raid shelters or in London the underground.
• Teams of wardens, **Air Raid Precaution wardens** (ARP), would keep watch on all public buildings and help fight fires. They formed teams of three to six people linked by phone to a control centre.
• The ARP wardens had the support of part-time firemen, **the Auxiliary Fire Service (AFS)**. The ARP and ARS worked with rescue squads and the ambulance service.

[He has dinner, and then about ten o'clock] I walked on to the Embankment [by the River Thames]. As I walked into the flashing night a bomb fell very near; near enough to deaden the world for a moment. Then came the noises of hurrying people: little crouching ghosts, moving against the crimson glow of the river. Flares fell in the east and the gunfire grew into wilder thudding than ever before. I think one knew that the forces were to be terrible.

I went back into the hotel... I suppose it was about half-past ten when the bombs began to fall like loosened hell. [midnight] Soon the night became scarlet. 'The docks' I heard somebody say. The scarlet sheet spread until it became a canopy, and the windows of the lofty warehouses caught the fire and flashed with ruby reflections, darting arrows of ruby and saffron light.

About half past one the bombs came nearer... Then I went down to the Embankment again. Two bombs had fallen across the river while I was away. The smell was strange, like the smell of steel against a grindstone, like stale mushrooms... Flames curled up from the opposite bank, and then I realized a danger that I had not thought of before. There was fire on the right and on the left, and I knew that if the flames came nearer, there would be no escape except by jumping into the scarlet water.

[He goes outside with a woman, 2.00] I think the most horrible thing was the sound of burning timbers. The cracking, malicious sound, like little devilish laughs. The fire and the tremendous towers of light were all so terrible and wonderful that one gazed at them like a child before a miracle. The sound of the fires was real. One hated that... [He grasps the woman's arm and they rush back inside, 2.15.]

[He was]... on the stairs when the bomb fell. The building staggered. One imagined that the vast stone structure was cracking, like icing sugar, and that one was living in the last second before death. Glass was flung at us, like hail through an open door. Then one

B

C

smelled falling masonry. I don't remember a cry or a movement from anybody. The woman said… 'You saved my life.'… We walked over rubble and glass - like cracked ice… [morning] Buildings we had known for twenty years were no more than cracked walls, with all the life that once breathed within them

collapsed into rubble. Little tongues of flame still licked the edge of great advertisements and the air was heavy with dust - a strange miasma [mist], rising from last night's hell. 99 **(A)**

(Hector Bolitho, *War in the Strand*, Secker & Warburg, 1942)

Blitz!

Prepare a radio broadcast on the night of 17 April.

1 Research (AT3)
Find out what you can about the Blitz, ARP wardens, the AFS, Morrison and Anderson Shelters, Civil Defence.

2 Squeezing the sources (AT3)
a Look at **C**. Say one thing that you would hear, see and smell if you were at the scene. What questions would you ask about what happened? Think what people might tell you about what had happened. Then draw up a class list of ideas, questions and answers.
b Read **A** quickly. What single word or phrase gets across the writer's message.
c Go through **A** slowly. On a copy, underline any words or phrases you do not know. Work out what they mean.
d Draw up a table about the night of 17 April (see below). Put in the columns the words and phrases

Hector Bolitho used at the times in the left-hand column and any you would add.

	Place	Heard	Smelt	Felt	Saw
9.00 p.m.					
10.00					
10.30					
1.30 a.m.					
2.00					
2.15					
Morning					

3 The broadcast (AT1, AT2)
a For the times above you can describe what you would have felt, seen, heard, smelt and tasted.
b Interview the following people: an ARP warden, an AFS member, the woman, a person in a bomb shelter, the hotel porter.
c Present your broadcast to the class.

ACTIVITY · ACTIVITY ·

The Home Front, 1939-45

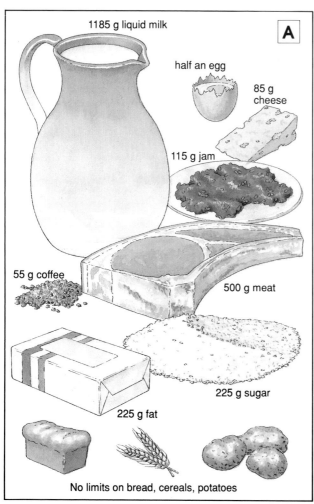

1185 g liquid milk

A

half an egg

85 g cheese

115 g jam

55 g coffee

500 g meat

225 g sugar

225 g fat

No limits on bread, cereals, potatoes

If you had been alive from 1939-45, the Second World War would have changed how you and your family lived. What changes were there in home life?

Rationing

The government was forced to act because the Battle of the Atlantic (see pages 44-45) saw U-boats sinking merchant ships that brought food to Britain. In January 1940 rationing began. Your family would get a ration book, which would allow you each week the amount of food shown in **A**. Other goods, like clothes and petrol, were also rationed. People would queue for hours for scarce food like lemons. The government got people to grow food on allotments. 'Dig for Victory' was a well know slogan (**B**). One way round rationing was to buy goods illegally on the 'black market'.

B

Gas Attack

The government was terrified that the Germans would use poison gas, one of the foulest weapons of World War I. So, every man, woman and child got a gas mask which they had to carry with them all the time. It was murder trying them on (**C**)!

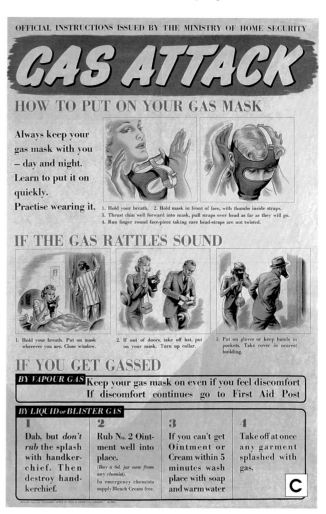

OFFICIAL INSTRUCTIONS ISSUED BY THE MINISTRY OF HOME SECURITY

GAS ATTACK

HOW TO PUT ON YOUR GAS MASK

Always keep your gas mask with you – day and night. Learn to put it on quickly. Practise wearing it.

1. Hold your breath. 2. Hold mask in front of face, with thumbs inside straps. 3. Thrust chin well forward into mask, pull straps over head as far as they will go. 4. Run finger round face-piece taking care head-straps are not twisted.

IF THE GAS RATTLES SOUND

1. Hold your breath. Put on mask wherever you are. Close window.

2. If out of doors, take off hat, put on your mask. Turn up collar.

3. Put on gloves or keep hands in pockets. Take cover in nearest building.

IF YOU GET GASSED

BY VAPOUR GAS Keep your gas mask on even if you feel discomfort. If discomfort continues go to First Aid Post

BY LIQUID or BLISTER GAS

1	2	3	4
Dab, but *don't* rub the splash with handkerchief. Then destroy handkerchief.	Rub No. 2 Ointment well into place. (Buy a 6d. jar now from any chemist). In emergency chemists supply Bleach Cream free.	If you can't get Ointment or Cream within 5 minutes wash place with soap and warm water	Take off at once any garment splashed with gas.

C

You never know who's listening!

CARELESS TALK COSTS LIVES

Secrecy

Fear of German spies meant that you would be on your guard (see **D**). You would not speak to strangers. Anyone in your family in the armed forces would take care not to tell you about what they were doing.

The Blackout

Fear of German bombing meant that your house would be 'blacked out'. No chink of light must escape from the windows, so for a time the sales of thick black material to line curtains must have soared! Cars also drove without lights - the result was that more British people died in car crashes than in fighting before D-Day!

Work

Many factories were busy with war work. The building of fighter planes was stepped up in 1940-41. The minister of aircraft production, Lord Beaverbrook:

> *appealed for scrap metal. Gardens lost their iron railings; kitchens lost their aluminium pots and pans. Labour regulations were ignored. Men in the aircraft factories worked 10 hours a day seven days a week.* **(E)**

(A.J.P. Taylor, *English History, 1914-45*, Oxford, 1965)

War Poster

We can use the headings on this page to research, design and produce our own war poster which should appeal to people to change how they live to support the war effort.

1 Thinking about change (AT3, AT1)
Study the text and sources. You can take one of these points, and report back to the class, or look at them all.
a What changes would happen to you today if:
• you had to have a diet based on **A**; work out your meals for a day or a week
• there was no petrol, and you had to queue for goods like bananas
• you tried to grow your own food on an allotment **(B)**
• you used your money to buy goods you wanted on the black market
• you had to carry a gas mask all the time and to try one on like **C**
• you had to take care about careless talk - what would you do if you heard someone talking about things which the Germans would find useful?
b How would you blackout your own home? How about walking around or driving at night!
c What changes might there be at work?
d How would Lord Beaverbrook's appeal affect your home **(E)**.

2 The poster (AT2, AT1)
Work on your own or as a group for your poster.
a Your poster should:
• have a heading
• include sections on Rationing, Gas Attack, Secrecy, The Blackout and Work.
b You can produce each piece on paper, cut them out and stick them on your poster.
c You can hold a class display of posters, and judge which is the best on these points: appeal, ideas, neatness, coverage of the main points.

ACTIVITY · ACTIVITY

The Home Guard

If tomorrow war broke out with a foreign power who was about to invade, how would you feel? From 1939-43 a German threat like this hung over your family.

After Hitler had overrun France in the summer of 1940 (see pages 36-37) it seemed likely that Germany would invade Britain. By August they had even got the barges ready to carry their troops across the channel. The British government set up a Home Guard with over a million men, many veterans of World War I. It had few rifles and little or no ammunition. It put up road blocks, dug ditches, checked identity cards and even made petrol bombs. The Home Guard trained hard (see **A** and **B**). I came across **C** in a wartime diary I was reading:

66 *I was admiring the gardens, with roses and camelias still in flower, when we turned a corner and*

came on a belligerent scene. A sturdy sergeant was instilling bayonet drill into a bunch of recruits. One of them, a small frog of a man, with spectacles, was treating his bayonet as if it were a pen in a bank. 'No', said the Sergeant, with contempt. 'Aim at his throat ...at ees throat!' War suddenly heated the little man's blood. He thrust his bayonet forward, his jaw so grim and his eyes so fierce that we instinctively drew back from the flame of his hate. I am sure that in the event of invasion, at least one German will fall back into the tide, with a nasty wound 'in ees throat'. **(C)**

(22 December 1941, Hector Bolitho, *War in the Strand*, Secker & Warburg, 1942)

On 7 September 1940 some church bells were rung, the signal that German paratroopers had landed. But it was a false alarm. Even little children's story books took up the theme of invasion. I was dead chuffed to find **D** while reading my young daughter her bedtime story. I always use it in my teaching:

Mole: 'Hare! You shall be the Home Guard'. You must defend Grey Rabbit's house and all our homes with your life... Squirrel, you must knit socks and stockings and mittens and scarves for all our fighters. Grey Rabbit! You must be a nurse and take care of the wounded.'

Hedgehog: 'What about me? I may be old but I can fight. I once killed an adder with my prickles.'

Mole: 'You are a brave fellow, Hedgehog. I shall want you to be a leader, a captain. Water Rat will guard the river banks. Wise Owl will fly over the woods and watch for the approach of the enemy. All the rest of the animals will be fighters, hidden on the war-path with bows and arrows, with pop-guns and swords and daggers. I shall dig a cavern underground where the young ones can hide in safety. **(D)**

(Alison Uttley, *Hare Joins the Home Guard*, 1940)

The Home Guard

How would you cope as a member of the Home Guard? Use the sources and what you can find out about the Home Guard to plan the defence of your school and the roads around it.

1 Finding out (AT3, AT1)

a Find out what you can about the Home Guard from other books and sources.

b What does the text and **A**, **B** and **C** suggest about:

- how a member of the Home Guard was dressed and why he was dressed in that way
- how he would be able to fight
- how the Home Guard was trained
- how the Home Guard would cope with an enemy tank attack

c List what **D** suggests men and women would do to cope with a German attack. Put them under two headings, Men and Women. Add other things that you have found out to the lists.

d You can interview people who lived through the Second World War. Work out your own questions, using what you have learned. Make out a group or class questionnaire. As a class you can pool the information you get back from the questionnaires.

2 Creating the Home Guard (AT1)

You can create your own form Home Guard.

a Work out who would do what jobs in it.

b Use a map of your school and the local area to work out how you would defend it from a German attack. Think about paratroopers, an infantry assault by 100 soldiers, how you would deal with an attack by three tanks.

3 The Home Guard (AT1)

Write a report with the title **The Home Guard** containing your answers to **1** and **2**.

Women in War

Today if you are a girl you expect to be treated in the same way as a boy: to have the same education, to have the right to do the same kind of jobs, to be paid the same and to live a full and happy life. Before 1939 most women were treated badly; only men really mattered. The Second World War brought about huge changes in the role of women. How? Why?

I worked out the *Factfile* and found sources **A-F** to help you think about women's wartime roles and the question, 'Did the war really change things?'

“ *The longer the war went on, the less publicized things like the ATA became. After a while the public didn't pay any attention to us. Sometimes we'd sit in a bar having a drink in our blue uniforms which had wings on them, and somebody might ask what service we were with… But everybody was doing something. People were digging people out of bomb holes, having a horrible time in icy-cold conditions. Ours was one of the nicest jobs you could have, flying all those wonderful fighter planes.* ” **(A)**

(Diana Barnato Walker, pilot, ATA)

“ *I was driving a crane and it was able to carry 20 tons. It was like driving a tram. I was always frightened that I would drop the drums because we had to go over these men who were working underneath… I was there from seven in the morning until seven at night. I worked with a lot of men and they thought that it was strange to have a woman drive a crane because it was so big.* ” **(B)**

C	Number of women workers	
	Agriculture	**Engineering**
1939	60,000	40,000
1943	220,000	700,000

FACTFILE
1940-41

- Most men from 20-41 were called up to serve in the armed forces.
- Women were needed to help with the armed forces and to work on the land and in industry.
- All women between 18-30 were called up to serve in the Auxiliary Territorial Service (ATS), the Women's Auxiliary Air Force (WAAF), or the Women's Royal Naval Service (WRNS), or to do war work (see **C**).
- Some 800,000 women were sent to work on the farms, in local government, industry, fishing or shipping.

The Armed Services
- Some 450,000 women in uniform by 1944. Women did the same work as men, including operating anti-aircraft batteries and sound locators **(D)**.
- Women in the Air Transport Auxiliary (ATA) flew Spitfires and other war planes **(A)**.

The Land
- On the land a land army was set up. Women played a key role as land girls **(E)**.
- By 1943 some 90,000 women were working on the land, doing the same work as men. Women did all kinds of farmwork, e.g. ploughed fields, milked cows, mucked out cowsheds, thinned turnips and harvested. Work was long and hard.

Industry, Building and Transport
- Women did the same jobs as men (see **B and F**).

74

During the war women had much more freedom than before. Husbands and boyfriends were away from home. Women's new jobs also gave them ideas of how they would like to live in the future.

When the war ended the men and their trade unions expected women to go back to the roles they had had before 1939. What do you think women felt about this?

Equal Opportunities

You can produce a **Women's Rights Charter** to show how women's roles changed in World War II and to argue that men and women should be treated equally.

1 Research (AT3)
a Find out what you can about women's roles in the Second World War.
b If you can, interview a man and a woman who were alive in World War II asking them what they remember about the role women played, and how it had changed from before the war.

2 Looking at the evidence (AT1)
Make out a table, using these headings, to show how the war changed women's roles:

	Jobs before 1939	In the war	Today
Text			
Sources A B C D E F			

3 Arguing the case (AT2)
Do you think the evidence shows that women's roles changed in World War II?

4 The charter (AT1, AT2)
Make out your charter to show what women achieved in World War II.

ACTIVITY · ACTIVITY

Yalta and Potsdam

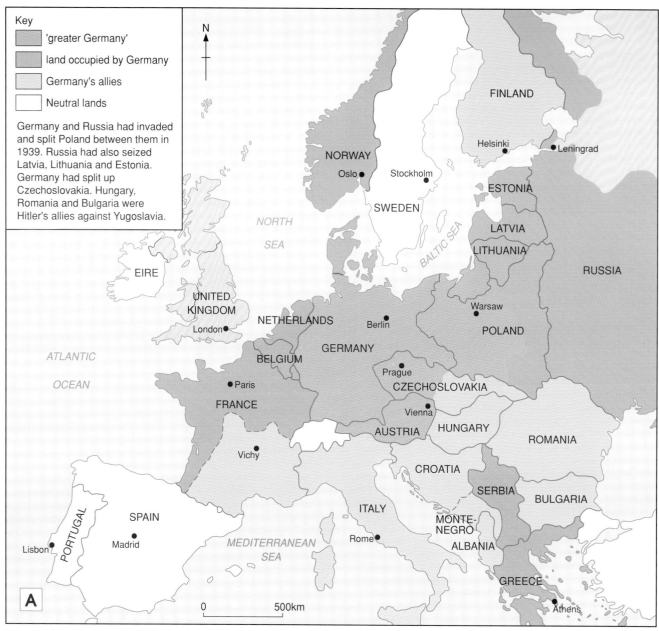

Key
- 'greater Germany'
- land occupied by Germany
- Germany's allies
- Neutral lands

Germany and Russia had invaded and split Poland between them in 1939. Russia had also seized Latvia, Lithuania and Estonia. Germany had split up Czechoslovakia. Hungary, Romania and Bulgaria were Hitler's allies against Yugoslavia.

A

Areas under German control in 1942.

The leaders of the three allied powers, America, Britain and Russia, met at Yalta in February 1945 and at Potsdam in July to work out a peace settlement that would follow the defeats of Germany and Japan. Map **A** shows the problems which faced the Allied leaders in Europe. Below are some of the plans they could have chosen.

Possible Plans for a Postwar Settlement

1 Eastern Europe

1a The countries have the same borders as before the war.

1b Borders are redrawn to take into account changes during the war.

1c Plan a, but Russia keeps control of Latvia, Lithuania and Estonia, part of Russia before 1919.

2 Germany - Borders

2a Germany returns to her pre-war borders.

2b The borders are redrawn to give Poland a secure border.

2c The borders are redrawn to give Poland land in the West in return for land Russia gains in the East.

3 German Occupation

3a Germany to be split up into four areas, each under one of the powers, America, Britain, France and Russia.

3b Germany to be under the joint control of the four powers.

3c Germany to have its own government.

4 Germans in Eastern Europe

4a They stay where they are.

4b They are forced to go and live in the post-war Germany.

4c Each country can decide to do what they like with their Germans.

5 German Leaders and War Criminals

5a They should be tried in each country.

5b There should be an international trial of them.

5c They should be shot without trial.

6 Russians and East Europeans who fought for the Germans and who are now in American and British prisoner-of-war camps

6a They should be handed over to the Russians to be sent back to Russia for almost certain death.

6b They should be allowed to stay in the West.

7 Reparations - Industry

7a Industry in the area of Germany under Russian control should be stripped bare and sent to Russia to rebuild the factories the Germans had destroyed.

7b All German industry should be stripped bare and sent to Russia to rebuild the factories the Germans had destroyed.

7c German industry should be left alone.

8 Democracy in Europe

8a The countries of Eastern Europe to have free, democratic elections.

8b The countries of Eastern Europe to have free, democratic elections under the control of the Russians.

8c Russia to set up communist governments.

9 International Peace

9a An international body, the United Nations, be set up to keep the peace, but with no army.

9b An international body, the United Nations, to be set up to keep the peace with an army.

9c An international body, the United Nations, to be set up to keep the peace with no army and with agencies to try and solve world problems such as refugees, famine, disease and poverty.

9d An international body, the United Nations, to be set up to keep the peace with an army with agencies to try and solve world problems such as refugees, famine, disease and poverty.

Other Problems

Peace Maker (AT1, AT2)

You can see how good an adviser you might have been to the three powers at Yalta and Potsdam.

a The class splits up into groups, at least three people to a group.

b Each person in a group takes the role of **one** of the powers at Yalta and Potsdam. Do this in alphabetical order of your surnames.

c For each point look at the map and use what you know about the state of Europe in 1945 to agree as a group on one of the plans *or* agree on a different plan for that point *or* disagree about the plan to be adopted.

d For each point write out what plan you came up with.

e For other problems work out a plan.

f Each group can report to the class on what its plans are for the peace. You can hold a class debate and agree on policies for each point.

g When you have finished your peace settlement look at the list below. It shows the things which were agreed at Yalta and Potsdam.

h Produce a report to suggest why your plans were better than those which the Allies came up with.

Plans most agreed on were: 1c, 2c, 3b, 4b, 5b, 6a, 7a, 8a, 9a.

ACTIVITY · ACTIVITY ·

The United Nations

Today if you switch on the radio or TV news you will hear or see stories which mention the United Nations. Jot down what you know about the UN, how it works and what it has done. The UN was set up in 1945. At that time the world's leaders had one main worry: how could they stop a conflict like the Second World War from breaking out again? Before 1939 most of the world's leading countries hoped that a body they had founded after the First World War, the League of Nations, would do this. The League of Nations was a ghastly failure - it had done nothing to stop Hitler. So, in 1945 America, Britain and Russia hammered out a new plan to keep the world at peace - they founded the United Nations. A huge problem was that Russia had already fallen out with Britain and America; the Cold War was about to begin (see **B**, which I felt summed up its causes very neatly).

How did the United Nations work? How well did it work? The spider diagram, **A**, should help you find out.

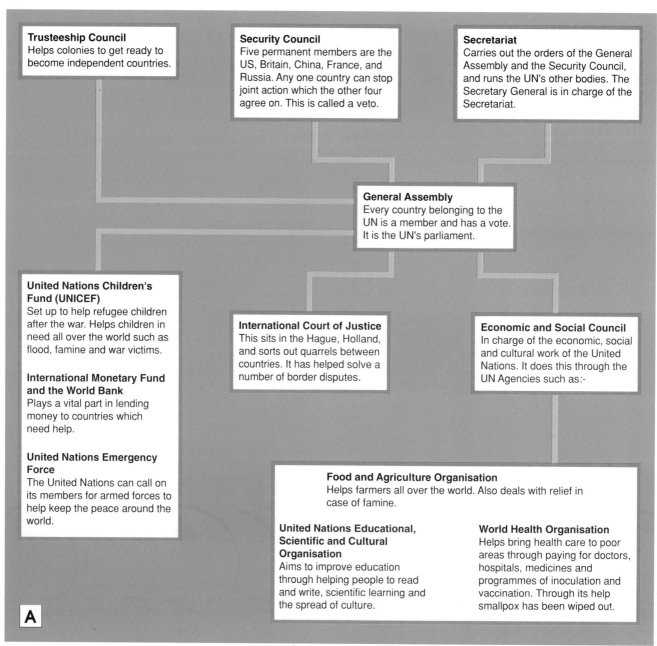

Trusteeship Council
Helps colonies to get ready to become independent countries.

Security Council
Five permanent members are the US, Britain, China, France, and Russia. Any one country can stop joint action which the other four agree on. This is called a veto.

Secretariat
Carries out the orders of the General Assembly and the Security Council, and runs the UN's other bodies. The Secretary General is in charge of the Secretariat.

General Assembly
Every country belonging to the UN is a member and has a vote. It is the UN's parliament.

United Nations Children's Fund (UNICEF)
Set up to help refugee children after the war. Helps children in need all over the world such as flood, famine and war victims.

International Monetary Fund and the World Bank
Plays a vital part in lending money to countries which need help.

United Nations Emergency Force
The United Nations can call on its members for armed forces to help keep the peace around the world.

International Court of Justice
This sits in the Hague, Holland, and sorts out quarrels between countries. It has helped solve a number of border disputes.

Economic and Social Council
In charge of the economic, social and cultural work of the United Nations. It does this through the UN Agencies such as:-

Food and Agriculture Organisation
Helps farmers all over the world. Also deals with relief in case of famine.

United Nations Educational, Scientific and Cultural Organisation
Aims to improve education through helping people to read and write, scientific learning and the spread of culture.

World Health Organisation
Helps bring health care to poor areas through paying for doctors, hospitals, medicines and programmes of inoculation and vaccination. Through its help smallpox has been wiped out.

A

Two points of view.

Moscow is Russia's capital. The man wearing the hat is Stalin. The figure holding up his fingers in a victory sign is Britain's leader, Churchill. The other person is America's president.

United Nations Rules OK?

How do you think the United Nations might work when faced with the problems of an imaginary country, **Utopia**, in 1946? Firstly read the Briefing, and then work out which agencies would act and what you think they should do.

Briefing
Utopia is on the borders of Russia.

1 The communist party is trying to seize power from the democrats, and a civil war has broken out between the communists and democrats. America and Britain back the democrats.

2 Utopia has a colony in the Far East, Subservia. In Subservia a revolutionary group has claimed that it should be independent.

3 A smallpox epidemic has broken out in Subservia.

4 Utopia's government is broke, and it needs some huge loans to get over its current problems and to build up its industry. The Germans had invaded it and blown up its mines and factories.

5 Subservia has no schools. Very few of its people can read or write.

6 Utopia has a huge number of peasant farmers. The country cannot grow enough food, although its farmland is among the richest in the world.

7 After the war a huge number of refugees flooded into Utopia. Among them are several thousand orphans. They live in squalid refugee camps without fresh water or toilets.

8 Russia claims that a border area of Utopia should be part of Russia.

1 Policy (AT1, AT3)
a Say which body in the United Nations would try and solve each problem mentioned in the Briefing.
b Put forward your own plans for dealing with each problem.
c Say what difficulties your plans might have.

2 The UN leaflet (AT1, AT2)
a Design a leaflet to teach eight year olds about how the UN dealt with Utopia. You can split the problems listed in the Briefing up among you.
b The leaflet will say why the UN was founded and what it does.
c The leaflet will have a sign or symbol for each body belonging to the UN, plus a caption of less than ten words about each.
d The leaflet will list how the UN might have dealt with Utopia's problems.

Refugees

1945. Germany lay in ruins. Europe was in chaos. The Russian army was in control of Eastern Europe and a huge area of Germany. The roads were choked with people fleeing from their homes. Soon the Russians were to force Germans living in Eastern Europe to go and live in Germany. Can you think why? **A** shows the size of the problem, while a report in November 1945 showed me what being a refugee meant:

> *Millions of Germans, Danzigers, Sudetenlanders* [Germans from these areas] *are now on the move. Groups of 1,000 to 5,000 will take the road, trek hundreds of miles, and lose half their numbers by death through disease or exhaustion. … One train, which arrived in Berlin on August 31st, started from Danzig on the 24th with 325 patients and orphans from the Marien Hospital and Orphanage in the Weidlergasse. They were packed into five cattle trucks, with nothing to cover the floors, not even straw. There were no doctors, nurses or medical supplies. Between six and ten of the patients in each truck died during the journey. The bodies were simply thrown out of the train.* **(B)**

(quoted in A. Howarth, *Twentieth Century History*, Longman, 1987)

War Story

Write a short story about being a refugee from Danzig.

Interview (AT3)
Base your story on an interview with a child from the train. Split into pairs, one person taking the part of an interviewer, the other the refugee. As a class, pool your answers to these questions:
• What had happened to your parents in the war?
• What was life like in the orphanage?
• What happened on 24 August (orphanage/station/train)?
• What went on in the cattle trucks?
• What happened when you reached Berlin?

2 Short story (AT1, AT2)
Write your short story from the point of view of the refugee.

Millions of refugees fled from their homes between 1939 and 1952.

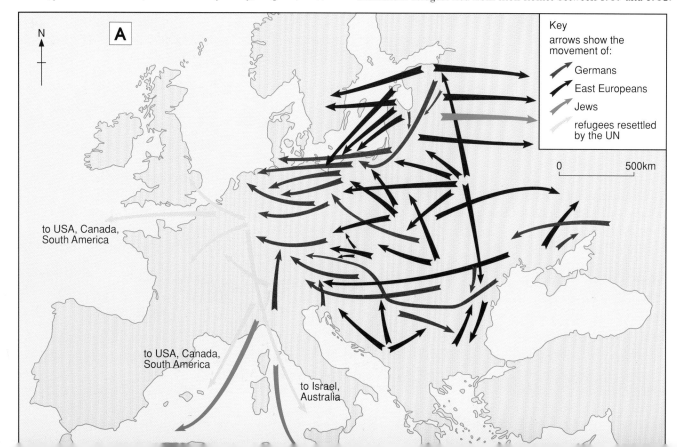